Getting started in Tales of Arise

How to make long and efficient combos?

One of the strong points of the combat system that all Tales of have in common is the ability to make spectacular and effective combos, and Tales of Arise is no exception. However, if this is your first game in the series, it can seem quite complicated to implement in practice. So here are our tips for making long and powerful Artes combos.

First of all, let's clarify what you can do (regardless of the character). At the beginning of the game, you can perform three normal attacks on the ground, three attacks in the air, and have three diamonds in your Artes Gauge (AG) that roughly represent the number of Artes you can perform. If you can no longer attack normally after making three normal attacks, you can continue to use Artes until this gauge is empty. It is very important to understand this last part because it is what allows you to extend your combos

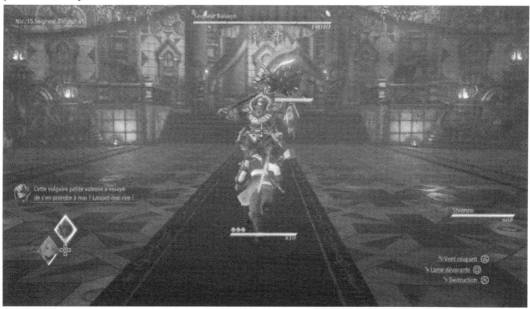

Indeed, each Arte consumes JA, and the consumption differs according to the power of the Arte (it is generally 1 or 2 maximum). So, we can already see a first possibility of combos quite long by following this path: Three classic attacks on the ground + Arte 1 JA + Arte 1 JA which propels in the air + Three classic attacks in the air + Arte 1 JA which brings the enemy back to the ground + Three classic attacks on the ground. Obviously, this is only one example among others and, above all, it is with only the possibilities of the beginning of the game. Some characters can do up to four classic attacks and 9 JA, which greatly increases the possible combinations and the length of the combos. These upgrades can be obtained by purchasing the skills from the Titles. Also keep in mind that the classic attacks are available again each time you go from ground to air and back again, so we usually try to include Artes that allow you to fly away or return to the ground.

Now, let's see how to make your combo. Because yes, in practice, the enemies are not going to stand in front of you and wait for you to chain them up without any resistance. That's why the best time to place your combo is when the enemy can't do anything. This includes the following situations:

When you have obtained a Break

After using a bonus hit that knocks the enemy down

After a counter-attack from a perfect dodge/guard This way, you will have plenty of time to perform your combos without being interrupted (although you should not forget that there are probably other enemies on the field who are not stunned and can therefore interrupt you).

Next, let's see how to set up your Artes shortcuts to perform your combos easily. Of course, this will depend on each player, but try to put some logic behind your shortcuts so you can remember them easily. For example, let's say your combo involves 6 Artes: 3 ground and 3 air, with the third ground being to propel into the air, and the last air to return to the ground. A possible and easy to remember set-up might be to start from the bottom up for the ground Artes (so in order Cross, Square, Triangle) and, once in the air, start from the top down (Triangle, Square, Cross) to keep the takeoff and landing intuitions you are trying to have with your combo.

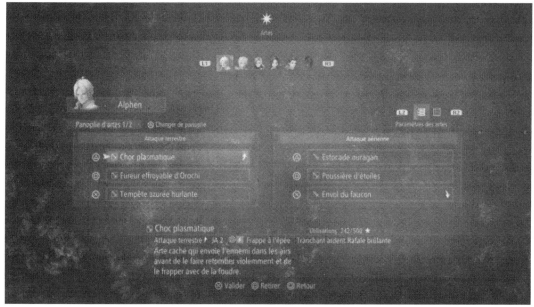

Finally, you will unlock towards the middle of the adventure the "Crocodile Crusher" artifact allowing you to set up 12 shortcut Artes (6 on the ground, 6 in the air). This will allow you to greatly expand your sequences and to diversify the Artes used.

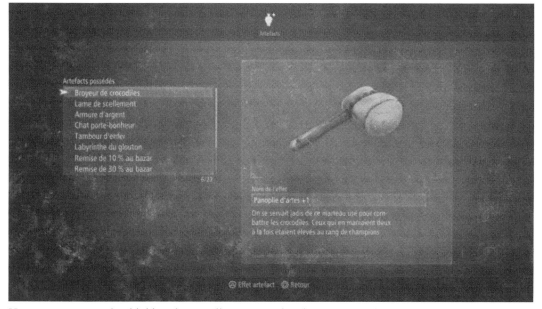

However, you may be thinking that you'll never get the chance to use that many Artes in one go since you'll run out of JA very quickly. That's where the Bonus Strikes come in. Each time you use a

Bonus Strike, your character gets 3 JA back. Bonus Strikes are an excellent way to avoid losing a combo in progress, since not only do you inflict damage when you perform the attack, but you also get back JA to continue using Artes. So don't hesitate to use the bonus strikes of characters whose bonus will not be used during the fight (for example, the enemy has no armor so Law's bonus strike is not very useful for this fight) to extend your combos.

How to set up your strategies?

In the Tales of, the actions of the three other characters you don't control are just as important as those of your character, if not more so. This is why it is essential to prepare your strategies well in order to adapt these actions to the situation

Fortunately, Tales of Arise allows you to set up some pretty deep strategies that will allow you to make the AI perform the actions you want. The game offers you almost a dozen predetermined strategies allowing you to order other characters to be aggressive or defensive, not to use items, or to heal in priority, no matter what.

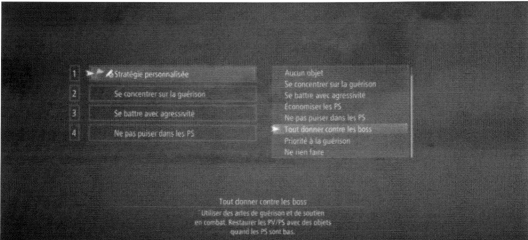

However, you should not hesitate to modify these existing strategies to make them even more

relevant to your needs. You can press 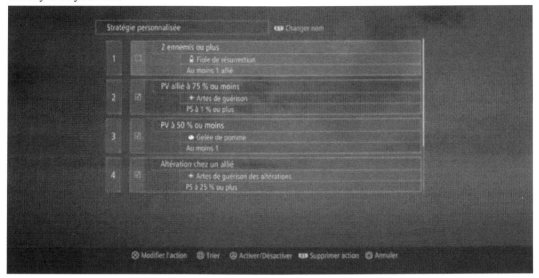 to obtain the details of the strategy in question, and modify it as you wish

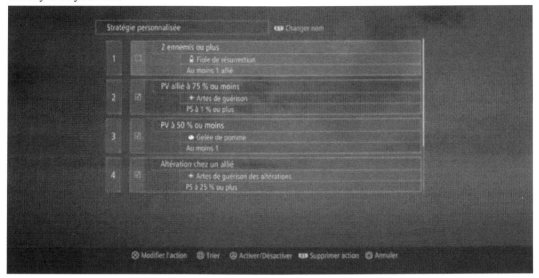

Once on the details screen, you will notice that the strategies follow the same principle as the "Gambits" in Final Fantasy XII. The first action is the one that will always be performed first if the conditions to perform it are met, then the second, and so on. For each action, you have three variables that can be adjusted: - When should the action be performed? (Number of remaining VPs, allies knocked out, enemies...) - What to do as an action? (Use an item or an arte...) - Adding a condition or a restriction for the action to be performed (optional, you can choose "No restriction" so that the action is always performed if possible)

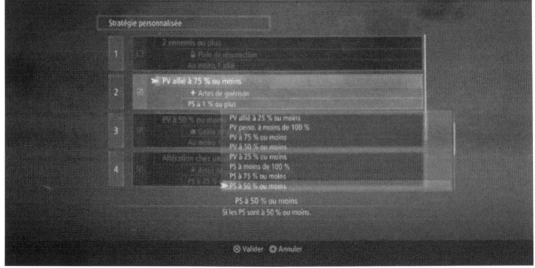

Again, it is highly recommended to customize all three variables to make your strategies even more relevant and effective. For example, the basic strategies generally give priority to artes to reanimate an ally. However, these artes are often long to throw, which can make them difficult to use in some fights. Saying that resurrection vials should be used instead may be more relevant. Also, some restrictions on items are useful to avoid wasting resources in fights against mobs, but problematic for boss fights.

You can even activate/deactivate actions directly so you don't have to spend time doing and redoing your strategies. This can be useful to prevent other characters from using buffs and support skills that are not relevant for the fight in question for example. Finally, you can change the order of priorities by simply pressing  .

While there are no perfect strategies for all situations, the strategy in the screenshot below is an example of a strategy that generally covers most battles well, whether for mobs or bosses. For the latter, however, you should not hesitate to modify it to fit the situation. There are only six actions, and the objective is to keep both the life level of the whole team and the healing points as high as possible in order to let the AI take care of the healing and allow you to be quite offensive on your side. However, it implies having at least Shionne or Dohalim in the team to work (although you can change the healing action to use items instead).

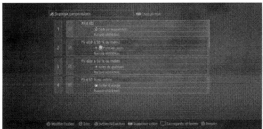

You can also add a "Stay away from enemies" action at the top, set to "Always" and "No restrictions" if you have mages and healers in your team to make sure they stay away from their target.

Care Points: How to manage them well?

One of the great new features of the Tales of Arise combat system is the introduction of Healing Points. Indeed, you have a healing gauge, visible in the menu and in battle, dictating the number of healing artes you can use. Managing these healing points is simply crucial since running out of them in the middle of a fight is usually synonymous with defeat.

If you're a series regular and this gauge worries you because it might prevent your favorite healer from standing in the corner and spamming healing artes to make you invincible, rest assured: it's still pretty easy to spam healing artes in the middle of a fight if you pay attention to certain conditions.

The first one is to always be careful not to run out of items to fill your SP gauge. You can have a maximum of 15 orange, pineapple and gold gels, which restore 30%, 60% and 100% of your SP gauge respectively. It becomes very easy to get 15 of these gels before every important fight (like Bosses and Giant Zeugles for example, which are the fights that will probably deplete your SP gauge the most). So, don't be afraid to set up your healer to spam the heals, and use these items as soon as the gauge starts to run low. To avoid going through the menu every time, add an action at the end of your strategy indicating to use a freeze to restore HP when the gauge is below X%.

 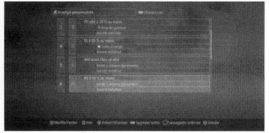

Although it is easy to fill up the SP gauge, this does not mean that you should waste SP. On the contrary, you should not hesitate to save them as much as possible, otherwise your resources will quickly melt away. There are several ways to do this:

Disable support actions that are not relevant to the fight: don't forget that buffs also consume SP. If you want your partners to stop using certain support skills, go to the Artes menu and deactivate the artes in question. There may also be an action in your strategy that instructs the partner to perform a certain arte when a certain situation arises. Deactivate these actions if they are unnecessary in the current situation.

Use items instead of artes to heal yourself: items have the advantage of not consuming any SP, and can be used immediately. Although using only items may cause a Jelly shortage very quickly, setting your strategies to use them only as a last resort (for a knocked out ally, near death, or a status alteration for example) allows a good balance between the two in order to devote your HP to basic healing.

Choose carefully the healing artes your healer uses: If the most powerful healing artes obviously heal more life, they consume a lot of HP. For example, Shionne's First Aid consumes 12 SP while Dohalim's Circle of Healing and Care consume 24 SP. If you see that the AI tends to overkill on heals and use spells that are too powerful for the situation, which destroys your SP reserve, don't hesitate to deactivate the most powerful artes to leave only the basic healing artes. Often, thanks to accessories, equipment or even cooking, the effects of the healing artes can be greatly improved, which makes the use of the first healing artes still relevant even when you are well advanced in the adventure. Also keep in mind that you can increase the power of the artes by repeating their use. At five stars, even Shionne's First Heal will heal your characters very well due to the quickness of the spell's casting, so don't hesitate to take a few minutes to farmer the use of the artes if necessary.

Outside of combat, mobs should not cause you to consume your gauge too quickly (unless you play on hard). Even if this is the case, there are always camps or inns where you can easily fill your SP gauge. So if possible, avoid using your jellies to fill up your SP gauge during exploration and save them for boss fights where the gauge may be depleted much faster.

Finally, don't hesitate to go hunting for giant Zeugles: Each victory against a giant Zeugle gives you an Astral Flower, an item that increases your SP by 10. Knowing that there are 20 giant Zeugles, that makes 200 additional SP possible (not counting the other astral flowers that can be found otherwise).

Manage your partners' AI well

In Tales of, the actions of your team are just as important as those of your character. However, there may be times when you bring a character into the fight to do a specific action, but you quickly realize that he or she almost never does it, which puts your entire strategy into question. Here are some tips that can help in this situation

CHECK YOUR STRATEGIES

Some of the game's predefined strategies are quite extreme, and if you haven't looked at the details of the strategy, it can cause your characters to behave in ways you didn't intend.

For example, the "Heal First" strategy encourages you to only use healing artes when an ally has less than 50% of their HP, and not to do anything else. Maybe this strategy was fine for your healer, but it applies to your whole team, even if the character has no healing artefacts, so he does absolutely nothing during the fight. So, before adopting a strategy, check the details to make sure it doesn't cause unwanted behavior from other characters.

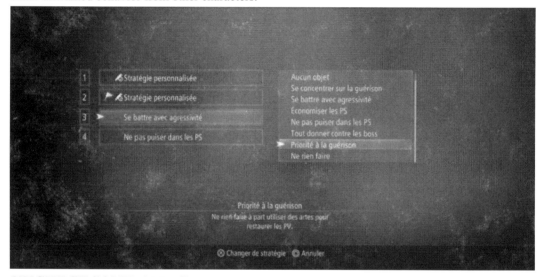

UNCHECK SOME ARTES

Preventing your partners from performing certain actions may seem counterproductive, but it is actually the best way to get the AI to do the actions you want. This is especially useful for healers and mages.

Let's say you want Shionne to only heal, without going through the strategies since this would influence the behavior of the whole team (be careful: your strategy must still have an action ordering to use a healing arte somewhere). You can simply discard all the non-healing artes, and Shionne will never be late to heal you again. Now let's say you want her to use only Circle of Care, and nothing else. Uncheck everything except Circle of Care and that's it, she'll only do that for the whole fight.

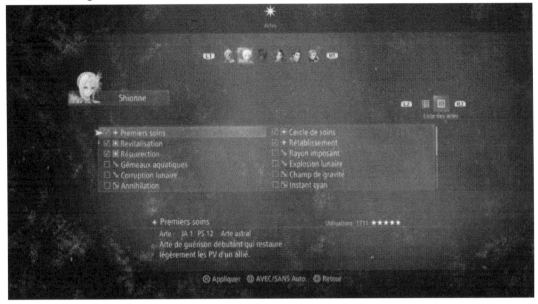

In the case of mages, it's also very useful to force them to exploit elemental weaknesses, or to use big area spells allowing a good "crowd-control" when you are facing several enemies. The logic is the same: if the boss is weak to light, unleash all of Rinwell's artes except those of this element, and she will have no choice but to spam these attacks.

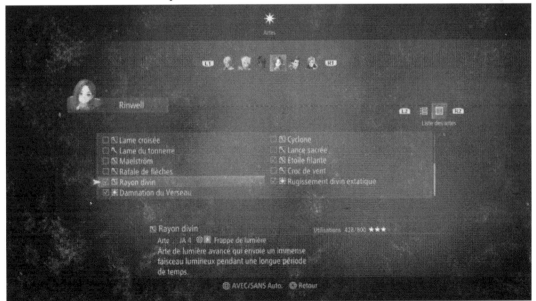

Be careful though, it's not really advisable to let your characters do only one arte (if they are supposed to hit in close combat). Indeed, they will have a lot of trouble making combos, and will tend to suffer the penalty applied when an arte is used several times in less than four moves.

CONTROL THE CHARACTER YOURSELF

You can change all the settings you want, there are some actions that the AI will never do as well as you. In fact, if you put a character on the team to perform certain actions but they can't, the best solution is probably to take matters into your own hands.

This kind of situation often happens with character strengths. For example, let's say the current boss you're fighting uses a lot of charged attacks. So it's more than appropriate to take Kisara on the team to benefit from her shield. That being said, if you're relying on the AI to make a perfect guard with Kisara, you can wait a long time. For this fight, it will be more relevant to control Kisara if you want to benefit from her strength to counter the charges. Don't forget that you can switch characters at any time, whether they are on the field or not, by pressing L1 and then the directional pad.

How do you cause disruptions and put the enemies on the ground?

One of the keys to the combat system of Tales of Arise is to manage to knock down the enemies to not only make them harmless, but also to inflict more damage. For this you have several solutions.

PROVOKE RUPTURES

First of all, it's worth clarifying something: breaking is not about knocking enemies to the ground, but simply about rendering them harmless for a short time. To put it simply, all enemies (and your characters, too, for that matter) have an Endurance stat. This stat is a kind of invisible gauge and, each time you take a hit, this gauge is emptied according to the Power of the hit (again, all enemies and your allies have a Power stat). Resistance and power are therefore two important stats that should not be neglected.

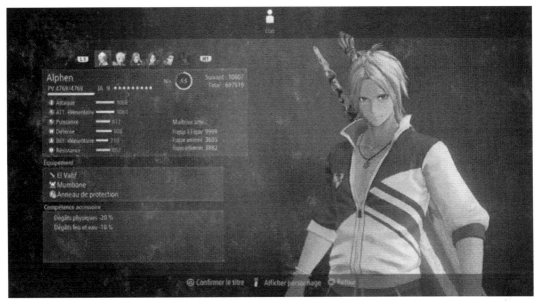

When this invisible gauge is completely empty, your enemy enters a state of disruption, meaning that the slightest blow will interrupt his action. In fact, if you don't benefit from the bonuses of attacking a downed enemy, just the fact that you can interrupt the enemy at will for a limited time makes some fights much easier. The enemy remains in the state of Break as long as you are able to keep the combo active: from the moment you lose it, the enemy returns to its normal state.

BONUS ATTACKS

The main advantage of bonus attacks is that each one can knock down an enemy and trigger various beneficial effects if the conditions are met. Indeed, all characters can knock down an enemy by fulfilling the following conditions:

- Shionne knocks down all flying enemies and keeps them on the ground - Rinwell can knock down an enemy charging a spell and steal the spell (single use of the stolen spell). In addition to stealing the spell, the enemy will not be able to use it for a while. - Law knocks down all enemies with protection (armor, carapace...) - Kisara knocks down an enemy charging if the timing is right. The bonus attack also increases the defense and elemental defense of all allies even if the attack is made in a vacuum - Dohalim knocks down fast enemies and prevents them from dodging for a while

Alphen is a special case since his Bonus Attack can knock down more or less all enemies regardless of the situation (except in case of Out of Bounds in general).

BONUS HITS

For each enemy, you will notice a kind of diamond-shaped gauge. This gauge fills up as you perform a long combo on the enemy. This gauge fills up very quickly but also empties very quickly, as soon as your combo usually stops. However, the lower your enemy's HP, the longer this gauge will stay full.

Once the gauge is full, you'll get a Bonus Hit by pressing the directional pad. In addition to knocking down the enemy, you will inflict huge damage. That's why you should try to do long combos to fill this gauge. This gauge fills up much faster when using unique Artes in a combo (except for mages).

Once you have the ability to add 3 more Artes to the ground and air, you will kill most of your enemies with Bonus Hits.

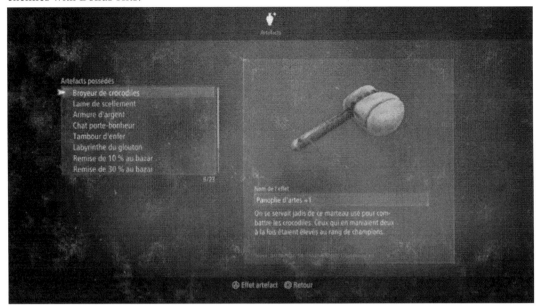

WEAKNESSES

Almost all massive enemies (Golem, Boss, Giant Zeugles) have a weak point. It is usually a very large orange crystal that you can't miss. This weak point must be your priority when you face this kind of enemy. Indeed, after inflicting a certain amount of damage, the crystal will break and your enemy will be on the ground. You can directly target the weak point with L1 (the key to select the enemy), which is very useful for melee characters.

Bonus Attacks

In Tales of Arise, each character has a bonus gauge in combat which, when filled, allows for a bonus attack. The bonus attack of each character has different effects that can be very useful if used at the right time.

As far as the bonus gauge is concerned, it fills up automatically over time during the fight for all characters, including those not participating in the fight. However, those who participate in the fight can fill it more quickly thanks to certain bonuses. Indeed, the more damage the character inflicts and the more counter-attacks he makes (perfect dodge + R1), the faster this gauge will fill up. This system rewards aggressiveness by allowing you to use these attacks more often.

A first advantage of these bonus attacks is that they allow you to get extra "free" damage, in addition to extending your combo. Indeed, when you use a bonus attack, your Arte gauge is full again. So don't hesitate to spam the artes in order to empty your Arte gauge, then use a bonus attack to fill it up, and spam the artes again in order to perform long destructive combos.

However, the main advantage of the bonus attacks is that each can knock down an enemy and trigger various beneficial effects if the conditions are met. In fact, apart from Alphen, who can knock down an enemy for sure, the other characters can knock down an enemy if the following conditions are met:

Shionne knocks down all flying enemies and keeps them on the ground

Rinwell can take down an enemy charging a spell and steal the spell (single use of the stolen spell). In addition to stealing the spell, the enemy will not be able to use it for a while.

Law knocks down all the enemies with a protection (armor, carapace...)

Kisara knocks down a charging enemy if the timing is right. The bonus attack also increases the defense and elemental defense of all allies even if the attack is made in a vacuum

Dohalim knocks down fast enemies and prevents them from dodging for a while

These conditions imply that it is sometimes better to keep a bonus attack in order to use it at the right time instead of spamming them as soon as they are available (Rinwell, Kisara, Shionne to some extent). Also, it can be interesting to integrate some characters according to the advantages of their bonus attack, especially against bosses, who have most of the time an obvious weakness against some advantages of the bonus attack of one of your characters (it is especially to fill the gauge more quickly, because he could very well do it alone otherwise).

Learn new Artes

In the Tales of series, in addition to the classic moves, you also have attacks called "Artes". These are the attacks that will allow you to make more impressive and efficient combos, to launch spells, buffs, or to heal yourself. If some Artes are learned naturally by advancing in the story or by leveling up, there are other ways to get new ones.

UNLOCKING SKILLS WITH TITLES

If most of the time titles allow you to unlock side effects, passives or bonuses, titles can also allow you to obtain new Artes. In general, Artes are not expensive in terms of CPs compared to other skills that quickly approach 1000 CPs. In fact, try to unlock as many titles as possible on your characters if you want to learn new Artes and expand your combos.

THE MASTERS OF ART

Sometimes, in the middle of a fight, a character will suddenly learn a new Arte. This is not a random event. In the description of your characters' stats, you will notice that each character has three types of mastery (different depending on the character) under the category "Arte Mastery". This mastery increases each time you use an Arte from this category.

For example, Alphen has "Sword Strike", "Air Strike" and "Flame Strike". So, each time you use the Arte " Mirage " for example, which is an air Arte, this counter will go up by 1, with a maximum of 9999. It is thus by making these three masters reach certain stages that you will learn new Artes.

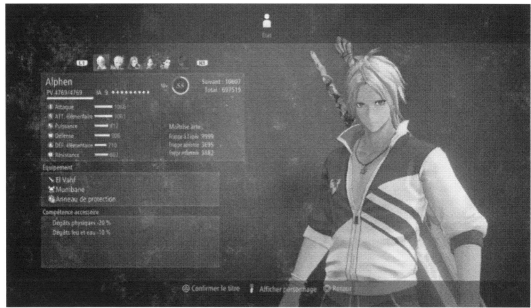

Maxing out the mastery is not as long as it sounds. Just by playing naturally, one of the three masteries will quickly reach 9999 depending on how you order your allies to play and how you play as well. Thus, it is very likely that Shionne will reach the maximum in healing before the end of the adventure.

If you want to grind Arte's mastery, you can use the same method as for grind Arte's uses, i.e. use the artifact "Sealing Blade" to do 1 damage and take an enemy with a lot of HP but with a much lower level than yours so that he is not a threat.

DO SIDE QUESTS

Side quests in Tales of Arise have many benefits: Money, PC, items, equipment... But they can also directly allow a character to learn a new Arte. They can also allow it in an indirect way, that is to say that, at first, it unlocks a new title for a character and, among the skills to unlock within this title, is a new Arte. However, it will never be directly stated in the side quest rewards that it allows you to obtain a new title.

Titles: How does it work?

Titles are back in Tales of Arise. They have a capital importance since they directly impact the statistical progression of your characters and give them many significant bonuses.

At the end of a fight, in addition to gaining experience, you will have noticed that you also gain CP (Skill Points). These CPs can be used to purchase skills available in each character's title. Each character has unique titles and therefore, unique skills (although many are similar). The bonuses are very diverse and varied: they can range from getting an extra JA, to improving the damage of the Bonus Hit, to making it easier to dodge perfectly. In any case, these skills are very useful in battle so don't hesitate to do side quests, a very good source of CP, to unlock as many skills as possible.

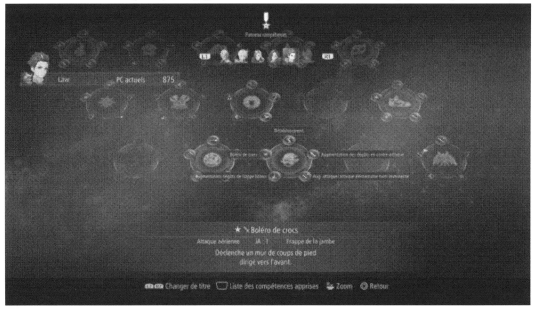

Each title gives you access to six skills, the first of which is automatically unlocked when you obtain the title. This means that you only need to buy five skills to unlock all the skills of a title. In general, it is always worthwhile to buy all the skills made available by a title because once you have obtained all six skills, you receive a statistical completion bonus. These bonuses vary depending on the title (and especially on the cost of the skills available within the title) and quickly become non-negligible since they can give up to +50 in a statistic

HOW TO UNLOCK NEW TITLES?

The first solution is to simply advance in the story. Indeed, your characters will get many titles by triggering certain story events so there should never come a time when you run out of skills to buy because you didn't get enough titles.

Another solution is to do side activities. "Side activities" obviously includes side quests, but not only. Fishing, ranching, the coliseum in Menancia, spending time with your allies after a campfire... All these activities allow you to get new titles, often with a particular character (for example, fishing allows Kisara to get a new title, healing people also allows it for Shionne...)

Cooking is also a source of many titles. This can manifest itself in different ways: cooking a certain dish with a certain character several times, getting a certain recipe and cooking it for the first time, preparing a favorite dish so many times... These are very easy titles to get so don't neglect cooking!

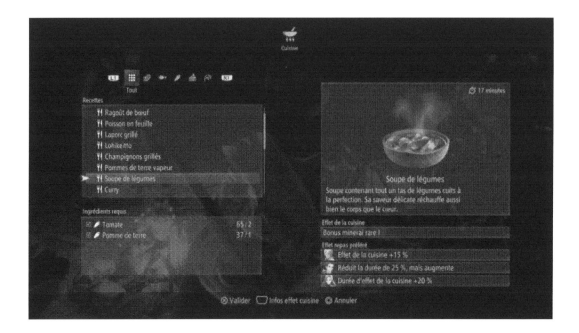

Off-limits and the Mystic Arts

As in every Tales of, in addition to the classic Artes, your characters can, if the conditions are met, perform super-powerful Artes called "Mystic Artes", allowing you to do super-powerful damage and conclude your combos in beauty.

HOW TO MAKE AN ARTE MYSTIQUE?

To be able to perform a mystical Arte, your character must be in an Out of Bounds state (which means you must be far enough into the story to have unlocked this mechanic). When this is the case, you must press two buttons that allow you to launch an Arte (no matter which buttons and no matter which Artes) at the same time. The last condition is that your Arte has to hit an enemy: you can't do an Arte in a vacuum and then press two buttons, it has to be in the middle of a combo, even if it's a one-shot combo.

In addition to being able to inflict enormous damage with these attacks, Mystic Artes can save you from dangerous situations. For example, if you are about to die and receive an attack, you can cast a Mystic Arte. This will interrupt the enemy's attack and put him back in the middle of the field.

OFF-LIMITS : HOW DOES IT WORK ?

We have seen that in order to perform a Mystical Arte, you must be in an Out of Bounds state: what does that mean exactly?

The Out of Bounds is a mechanic that is automatically triggered during a fight on a character. In simple terms, it is an invisible gauge (i.e. there is no way for the player to see how full it is) that fills up according to two factors: damage received and perfect dodges/guarding. When it is full, the character enters Out of Bounds. A blue bar then appears above your life bar to show you how much time you have left in this mode. Some title skills allow you to extend the duration of Out of Bounds.

You have many advantages in Off-Limits. First, your Artes can no longer be interrupted, which is extremely advantageous for mages and healers. Beware, you can still take damage and the penalty for using the same Arte in less than four moves still applies. The off-limit is not an excuse to rush in without thinking. Secondly, the damage received is reduced and the damage inflicted is increased, allowing you to be much more offensive. Finally, as we saw above, this is the only way to perform Mystic Artes.

While these perks are very useful when applied to your characters, they are much less useful when applied to the enemy. All bosses and giant Zeugles can enter an Out of Bounds state. This usually happens once they lose half their life, but some bosses can do it at any time.

The situation can quickly become critical when a boss enters Out of Bounds. Not only do they hit harder, receive almost no damage, cannot be interrupted or knocked down (even with Bonus Hits), they also become much more aggressive and some have access to new and more dangerous attacks. In the case of lords and bosses of major importance in the story, they can even perform Mystic Artes. When this happens, it's best not to be on the offensive and instead just dodge the enemy's attacks while waiting for the storm to pass, because if you try to fight them head-on at that point, you'll most likely regret it quickly.

Fight to gain more experience

In Tales of Arise, there is a system of Bonus of chain of fights allowing you to gain more experience and skill points (CP) according to the chain of your fights. This system takes the form of a 5 level multiplier which is indicated by the yellow gauge on the right of the screen. Simply, at level 1, the multiplier is 1.1, at level 2, 1.2 etc. up to 1.5.

In order to increase this multiplier, you just have to fight one battle after another. This will fill up the gauge, and you can move on to the next level when it is finally full. The speed at which the gauge fills up depends on three factors: the number of enemies faced, the level (compared to your own), and the difficulty chosen by the player. In other words, if you face a group of 5 enemies, with three levels more than your team, on hard difficulty, you will probably get a multiplier of 1.4 right away, while if you face two enemies below your level in Normal, it will take you several fights before you reach level 1.

When you reach level 5, the gauge turns blue. It will then empty very quickly, and you will only have about ten seconds to be able to continue fighting and keep the 1.5 multiplier active. If the gauge empties, you will start from 0, while for the previous levels, you will only have gone back to the lower level but will still have an active multiplier.

To take full advantage of this system, don't hesitate to crank up the multiplier to the max just before a major fight (boss and giant zeugle) to get a ton of experience and PC. By doing this, you'll probably never need to grind, without finding yourself completely overleveled (it's only a 1.5 multiplier after all). If you ever see that the multiplier at level 5 is about to disappear, you can always use a 1 Happy Vial to refill it. If you don't want to waste time fighting to fill up the gauge to level 5 just before a boss fight, you can simply use 3 Happy Vials to have the gauge at maximum.

Perfect dodges and perfect guards

In Tales of Arise, successfully dodging enemy attacks at the right time triggers a "perfect dodge". Unlike a normal dodge, which simply avoids taking a hit, a perfect dodge has many advantages that should not be overlooked.

Firstly, just after a perfect dodge, you will be able to perform a counter-attack on the enemy you are aiming at (not the one attacking you, because you can perform a perfect dodge of an enemy's attack even if you are not aiming at him) by pressing the classic attack button. Beyond doing damage, this attack will interrupt him as if he was in a state of Rupture, and thus leave you the possibility of linking on several Artes and creating a combo.

Absolutely all attacks can be dodged perfectly, be it physical attacks, charges, spells, projectiles, even mystical artes and the distance to your opponent doesn't matter since you will be directly teleported in front of him once the counter-attack is done.

If the timing of perfect dodges is a bit scary, you should know that several titles for each character give access to skills that make perfect dodges easier, i.e. the timing is less severe. In other words, a dodge that would have been normal before because it was made too early or too far away will now be a perfect dodge. The effect is cumulative between these skills, so that the timing becomes easier and easier to have, to the point where you will make perfect dodges without really doing it on purpose, especially on big area attacks and spells.

As for Kisara, who, as a reminder, guards instead of dodges, the principle is exactly the same. By making a perfect guard (just when the enemy is about to touch you), you will have the possibility to counter-attack. Kisara's particularity is that when she makes a perfect guard, you will notice an aura around her. This aura means that the power of her Artes is increased and they are more difficult to block. Also, she has skills that make it easier for her to time her perfect guard.

Farmer the use of the Artes and the Mastery of the Artes

Like all the games in the Tales of series, Tales of Arise rewards you when you use the same Arte many times. Indeed, the more you use an Arte, the more powerful it will become. If farming can seem intimidating, there is a trick to make it much easier.

The use of the Artes can be seen on the Artes selection menu of your characters. To the left of the name of the Arte, you will notice a section Uses with a ration X / 100 for example, and 5 stars. This means for example that in order to get the level 1 of the use rank of this Arte, you will have to use it 100 times. With each rank the Arte becomes stronger, i.e. it will do more damage if it is offensive, heal more HP, the casting time will be shorter if it is a spell, the time the stat increase lasts increases if it is a buff etc. If the difference may seem small at first, it is significant if you compare an Arte at level 0 and the same Arte at level 5 (so with 5 stars).

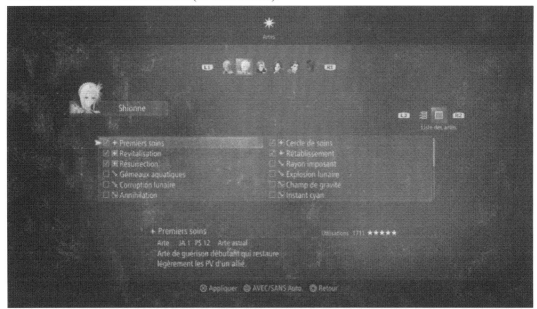

For example, Shionne's "First Aid" (the very first healing spell in the game) will heal more HP than "Revitalization" at level 0, even though it is supposed to be one of his best healing spells, and it is much faster to cast. To farm the use of a particular Arte, you have several solutions: one for the short term and another for the long term.

The first one is pure farm. You will simply go into battle, redoing the same Artes hundreds of times. Yes, it's not very exciting, but with a little trick, it can go pretty fast depending on the Arte. The goal is not to kill the enemy. To do this, you can use the artifact "Sealing Blade" which allows you to do only one damage with each hit. Then, start a fight with an enemy who has a lot of HP but whose level is much lower so that he doesn't pose any danger and can't interrupt your Artes because his Power is too low compared to your Resistance. All you have to do is repeat the Arte over and over again. Be careful though, the Arte must touch the enemy for the use to count: you can't stand in a corner and do Artes in a vacuum.

The second is to let the AI do the work for you when you play naturally. For example, if you want to farm Rinwell's Crossblade use, you can uncheck all her other Artes so that she can only do Crossblade all the time. This way, you'll be farming the uses without really feeling like you're farming and doing something else, which is probably more enjoyable. You can even combine the two methods to be even more efficient, i.e., untap all the Artes except the one you want to farm on your other three characters while you do it yourself on the character you control.

Since, with these techniques, you are pranking the use of the Artes by using them, you are at the same time pranking the Mastery of the Artes, so you are killing two birds with one stone.

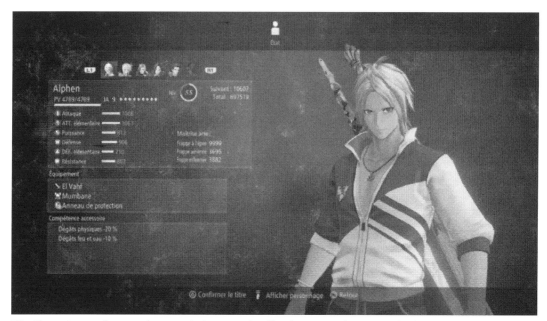

Finally, you can also use the game's Auto mode allowing your characters, including the one you are supposed to control, to play by themselves. Be sure to take an opponent with a lot of HP but posing no threat, uncheck all the Artes except the ones you want to level up, and let the console run while you do something else to farm without wasting your time.

Friendship with allies: How to unlock the second Mystic Artes?

If your allies have a first mystical Arte, it is also possible to unlock a second, even more powerful one, by forging a strong friendship between Alphen and the other team members. Here's how to do it.

When you are camping, just before your characters go to sleep, you will be asked if you would like to talk to a team member. Talking to your allies will strengthen the friendship between Alphen and the teammate you talked to. Once the friendship with a character is at its maximum, you will unlock his or her second Mystic Arte.

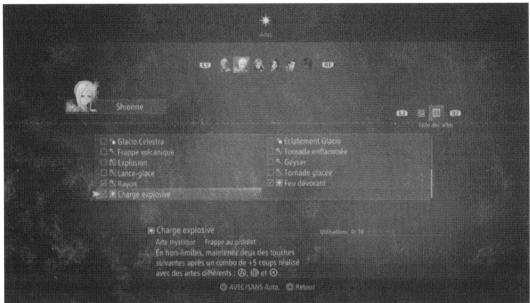

However, it is not enough to camp in a loop and talk to them randomly to improve the friendship. In fact, the friendship only progresses if the teammate has something to say, which is indicated by three small dots in a dialog box. By selecting the character concerned, you will then have a skit with a message at the end saying "you are closer with X". If this dialog box is not present, then talking to him is useless. In fact, if no ally has anything to say, you can sleep right away. Also, once the relationship is over, a small smiley appears, which means that there is no point in talking to him anymore.

To make these dialog boxes appear, you have to wait about 1 hour (in real life, not 1 hour of play) and to have been at least a little active, i.e. to have done some fights since the last discussion. Knowing that there are about 6 scenes for 5 characters (since Alphen doesn't count), the best way to progress quickly in the friendship of your allies is to take care of them from the beginning little by little. Every time you play, after about 1 hour, go back to camp to see if new dialogues are available. This way, you will get all the second mystical artes of the allies well before the end of the game.

The kitchen

As in all Tales of, cooking is very important in Tales of Arise. Cooking food in inns or camps allows you to benefit directly from various stats boosts in battle for a while, and should therefore not be neglected.

Let's face it, there's absolutely no reason not to have an active meal all the time. The benefits are simply too great to ignore. This is even more true for boss fights: make sure you always cook before you go into a major battle. You always have inns or camps nearby (or use fast travel) so take advantage of them!

The benefits and their power vary depending on two things: the dish being cooked, and the character cooking the dish. The effects provided by the dishes are very diverse: attack bonus, defense bonus, elemental damage bonus, drop bonus, EXP bonus... there is always a dish that meets your needs. You can get new recipes by collecting new ingredients, finding them in chests, or by doing side quests. Always be on the lookout for new ingredients and recipes in order to gain a significant advantage during the most important battles.

As for who cooks, this directly impacts the power of the effect of the dish. In general, each dish is the favorite of one member of the team, which results in having certain advantages if it is cooked by that member. The same dish can be the favorite of several characters, but with different consequences.

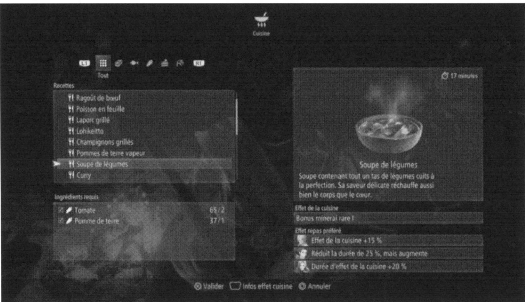

You also don't have to have the dish cooked by someone who prefers it, since this may have the opposite effect to what you want. For example, a character's cooking bonus may increase the duration of the dish, but decrease its effectiveness by 20%. If you are about to face a boss, this is probably not what you want.

Team Members' Guide

Alphen

In keeping with the traditions of the series, each playable character in Tales of Arise has very distinct characteristics and the way to play each of them is therefore very different, as you have to take into account their strengths and weaknesses. Let's first look at how to play the main character of the game, Alphen.

Like all the main characters in the Tales of, Alphen is the easiest character to pick up and control, and you can get away with doing the whole adventure with him (although it would be a real shame to miss out on the strengths of the other team members).

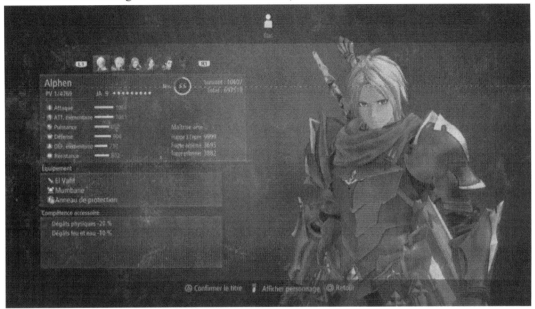

The fact that this is a mainly melee character makes it easy to learn basic combos. It is particularly useful for learning the synergies between ground artes that send the character into the air, air artes that extend the combo into the air, and finally air artes that send the enemy back to the ground. For example, you can start with a few basic attacks, Devouring Blade/Demonic Fang for a first arte, Flight of the Wyvern to send the enemy into the air, again a few basic attacks then Hurricane Strike to keep the enemy in the air, then Mirage/Falcon Flight to send the enemy back to the ground and repeat the operation.

While Alphen's basic artes are already very interesting, their 'fiery' version, Alphen's forte, is even more spectacular. After using an Arte (ground or air), you can hold the key to trigger the strong point and launch the 'fiery' version of the arte. These are usually much more powerful versions, with the elemental affinity of fire, and will usually cause enemies to falter very quickly. It should be noted that this version of the Arte will usually have the opposite (or neutral) role of the basic Arte, but rarely the same. For example, if Envol de la wyvern allows you to send the enemy into the air, Envol du Phoenix sends him straight back to the ground.

The major counterpart of Alphen's strong point is that to trigger the "fiery" version, it is necessary to sacrifice HP each time you use it. While this sacrifice should not be overlooked, it should not discourage you from using his strong point. Indeed, the more HP you sacrifice, the more damage you will inflict. With certain skills activated, you will be able to sacrifice almost your entire life bar to inflict simply enormous damage, and will melt the life bar of the bosses. You really shouldn't hesitate to sacrifice as much health as possible, even if it means being down to 1 health. After attacking, you can simply back away to take cover, and wait for an ally to heal you, or even use an item if you're really afraid of dying.

This is even more effective when you perform a fiery version of an Arte on a downed enemy. Alphen's Bonus Strike allows you to knock down any enemy, without any conditions. So, as soon as your Bonus Strike is available, make sure you have full life, knock the enemy down and sacrifice all your HP. If the damage would have been impressive in the first place, it will be even more so here as the enemy is down, making your hits even stronger.

Shionne

Shionne is simply the best healer in the group (there is not much competition, admittedly), with direct access to "First Aid", reanimation with "Resurrection" and healing for altered states with "Recovery". However, when you control it, you should not hesitate to delegate the healer role to someone else (Dohalim for example, or use items) because playing the role of the team healer in a Tales of, probably doesn't interest you.

Fortunately, Shionne is also very interesting offensively. She can attack enemies from a distance without having to wait to cast a spell like Rinwell and Dohalim (although she also has such artes). Her firearm allows her to be very effective against airborne enemies, and easily knocks them down with her artes involving her rifle.

Generally speaking, Shionne's ground-based artes are very diverse: ranged attacks, spells, healing, but also explosive strikes, a type of attack that is exclusive to him. Shionne has the ability to throw grenades, often elemental, which allow you to complete your combos and inflict status alterations. If simply throwing the grenade allows you to launch a first attack, you can unleash a much more devastating attack by holding the key. There is often no point in not charging the grenade, so be sure to use the attack at the right time during your combo as this slight loading time must be taken into account.

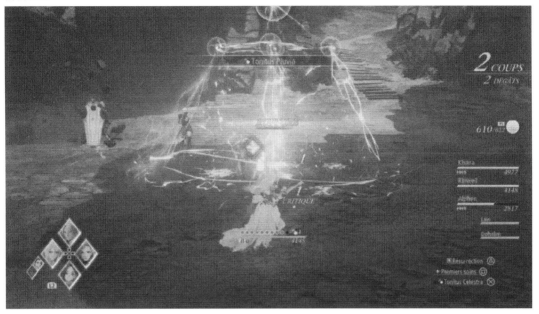

Another factor to consider when using grenades is that Shionne has a stockpile of grenades, the number of which can be seen in the top right of her life bar. When she runs out of grenades, Shionne can still use the primary version of artes with grenades, but she must first reload to use the higher version. To do this, you can either perform a basic attack once your supply is empty, in which case Shionne will reload before attacking, or reload at any time by pressing L2 and R1 at the same time.

Last but not least, Shionne is the best way to inflict state alterations on enemies, including bosses. Indeed, many skills in her titles allow her to increase the rate of alterations, and for reminder, these skills are cumulative. Similarly, most of his Elemental Artes have the side effect of inflicting alterations. With access to Fire, Water, Darkness, and Light Artes, Shionne can inflict poison, curse, freeze, and paralysis. Knowing that these alterations can be stacked on a single target, you can quickly render overpowered bosses completely harmless.

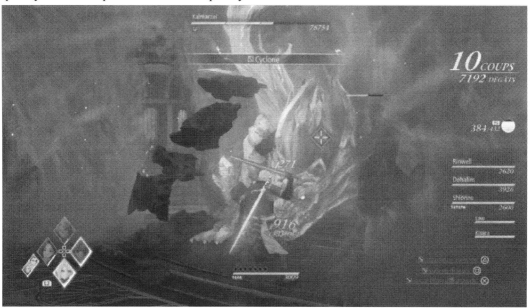

Rinwell

Rinwell is obviously the black mage of the team. She has a large number of elemental attacks, which makes her particularly useful for exploiting elemental weaknesses.

As far as ground-based spells are concerned, most of them are elemental spells that require a certain amount of time before they can be cast, depending on their power. For this type of spell, it is generally advisable to move as far away as possible from where the enemies are so as not to be threatened by the opposing attacks when you take the time to cast a spell. Unlike the old Tales of however, you can move while a spell is loading (you need to unlock the corresponding skill), and most importantly you are not immediately interrupted when you are attacked, which makes it easier to get the hang of the character.

Unlike its ground artes, its air artes have no loading time and are more likely to complement a combo initiated by your allies or a ground arte. These artes also have an elemental affinity allowing you to continue to exploit weaknesses. The idea is to complement ground artes, which are generally massive and destructive attacks with air artes or other ground artes but which are more likely to be used in close combat to create combos with Rinwell.

However, to be able to do very impressive combos with Rinwell, you have to use his strong point. Indeed, if you hold down the key when you cast a spell, you can delay the casting of the spell. Now, if you press R1 (basic attack key), Rinwell will store that same spell and charge it. What this means in practice is that when you go to use another spell, Rinwell will cast that spell first, then the stored spell, and this is what makes for really big combos and wobbles.

Even better, this technique allows you to cast overpowered artes that you probably don't have access to yet. This is possible by casting the loaded version of the spell. To do this, either cast the same spell twice (if you store Air Shock, then use Air Shock again, you will cast Cross Blade), or store a spell of one element, then cast another higher ranked arte of the same rank. For example, if you store Air Shock, then use Cross Blade, you will cast Cyclone. The latter method is probably the easiest way to cast destructive spells with Rinwell, as you can store a beginner's arte very quickly, which takes a short time to charge, and then cast an intermediate arte to activate a super-powered arte.

Note that this technique is also possible for Rinwell's support skills. For example, if you first store Acuity, then use Acuity again, you will launch the buff on the whole team. Be careful though, don't forget that support skills also consume SP, and these buffs are very greedy so you shouldn't abuse them too much, at least at the beginning of the game when your SP gauge is limited.

One of the big advantages of Rinwell is that his most powerful spells are very massive attacks that cover almost the entire arena, which has the following benefits:

- They are very difficult to avoid, very useful against very mobile enemies

- They allow to eliminate the mobs accompanying the bosses very quickly
- They allow you to hit the weak points (orange core) of the bosses without any risk since you attack from a distance. If the enemy has several, you will hit them all, which is even better.

If you don't like playing as a mage, but still want to keep Rinwell on the team, consider setting the "Stay away from enemies" action in your strategy, with "Always" and "No restrictions" so that she stays as far away from enemies as possible when she casts her spells (be careful, a strategy applies to all your allies, so be sure it doesn't interfere with the behaviour of your other characters)

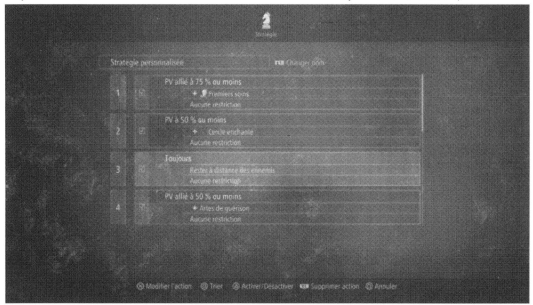

Law

Like Alphen, Law is a primarily hand-to-hand character, with a few supporting artes to either maintain his life or his offense. Because Law's moves are so fast and powerful, he easily wobbles enemies and allows for quick bonus hits, especially if he exploits elemental weaknesses. This makes him a very simple character to learn how to do long and powerful melee combos.

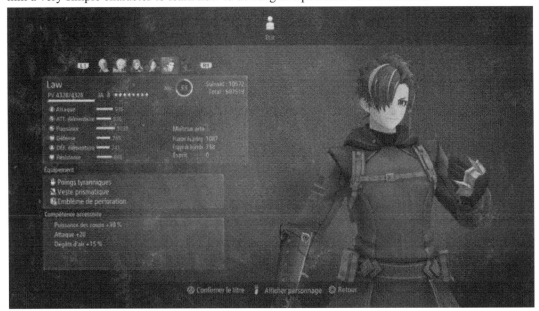

Thanks to his strong point, his physical and elemental attacks become even more powerful, and he can even more easily make enemies stagger and get bonus hits. To trigger his strong point, all you have to do is to perform a certain number of attacks without being hit. A blue and then yellow flame then appears around his hands and feet to indicate that the strong point is active, with the yellow light providing an even more powerful boost than the blue light.

This power point remains active as long as Law is not hit, but can stop if a certain amount of time passes without you managing to hit the enemy (sometimes, even if you get hit, the aura does not disappear). In fact, it is necessary to be very aggressive when controlling Law, but it is also necessary to be careful not to get hit in order not to lose the bonus. Taking damage is often very bad with Law because, in addition to losing the bonus, Law has very bad defences, so it is not uncommon to see him die very quickly, especially if you leave him to the AI.

Law's elemental covariance is very interesting, and makes Law probably the most versatile character on the team since he can cover all weaknesses except for Darkness. With his Steel Arte buffing his attack and elemental attack by 30%, Law is clearly one of the best at exploiting elemental weaknesses among physical characters.

In short, if all you want to do is hit monsters the old fashioned way with your hands and feet, with simple combos that do a lot of damage, Law is clearly for you character. However, be careful not to fall into the trap of being too gruff because if you are not able to dodge, Law will not last long in battle.

Another problem with Law is that if you don't control him yourself, the AI is not good enough to dodge attacks regularly. This has several negative consequences: - On the one hand, Law will rarely be able to use his strength and have attack boosts since the AI will regularly lose him - Due to his low defense and HP, he will be knocked out quite often, especially in the higher difficulties.

Kisara

If you like counter and parry mechanics, this character is for you. Kisara is basically the tank of the team, with average offensive skills, but which can be improved with well executed parries, and with incomparable defences. Her main gimmick is the fact that, unlike all other team members, Kisara does not dodge but uses her shield to parry and defend.

In fact, she excels against all enemies that have one or more charge attacks, and there is really no reason not to include her in the team (or even play her) when facing this kind of enemy. Indeed, if you defend when an enemy is about to charge you, you will perform a perfect defence, which will directly knock the enemy down. A yellow light also appears around the shield to indicate that your artes now do more damage and are harder to block.

Some artes like Lion's Roar also become even more powerful if you perform them with the guard up. These artes should be used to counter enemies and initiate your combos, so that you can follow up with more classic artes.

Surprisingly, Kisara also has a few support and healing spells (Protective Aura for example), which can deal damage while healing/helping your team. These spells should be seen more as a way to counter enemies than a way to heal yourself, Kisara will never properly replace Shionne and Dohalim for healing.

Dohalim

Dohalim is more or less a jack of all trades: he has Melee, Healing, Spell and Support skills. A character with such diversity has several advantages.

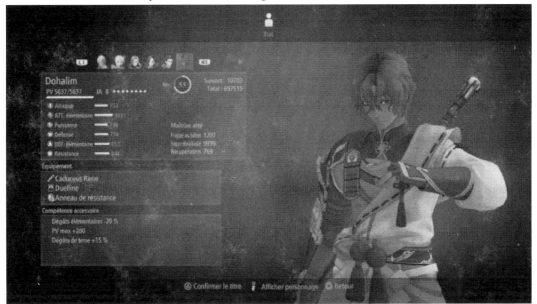

At first, he can take over the role of another character while the latter does something else. For example, if the boss you're fighting is a bird, you'd better use Shionne offensively, and Dohalim can take care of him. In the same way, he can come and help another character in his role (assist Alphen and/or Law in close combat, or Rinwell by casting spells for example).

Dohalim is also interesting because of his strong point. Whenever you make a perfect dodge, his staff extends in the same way as Leia in Tales of Xillia. When his staff is extended, not only does he have a longer range, but his attacks will more easily interrupt enemies, and his critical rate increases. The beneficial effects of the elongated staff can be greatly enhanced by the many skills available with its various titles (more damage, increased critical hit rate, longer duration...).

To perform combos with Dohalim, you can for example start by casting a spell that requires a loading time, which will probably cause the enemy to wobble, before moving on to physical artes. Like Law, being able to dodge attacks is necessary to get the most out of your abilities.

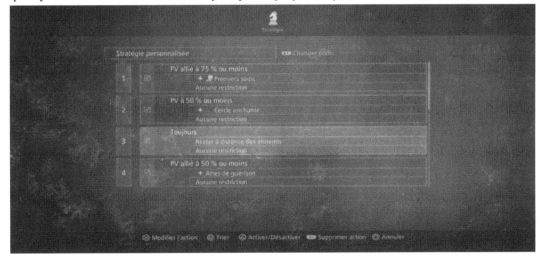

As a mage, Dohalim is very efficient. He is also the only one, along with Shionne, to have access to the Dark Arts. Thus, a very interesting strategy to implement if you do not wish to play Dohalim directly is to form a team with three mages: one white mage (Shionne) and two black mages (Rinwell and Dohalim). Add a "Stay away from enemies" action with the conditions "Always" and "No restrictions" to make sure that all three stay away from enemies to cast their spell. You, meanwhile, play a physical character who acts as a decoy for the enemies. This way, your mages can quietly bombard the enemies while they desperately try to hit you.

Les Artes

List of Artes d'Alphen

Arte	Master Arte	Element & direction	Fiery edge
Devouring blade	Swordsmanship	-	Infernal torrent
Demonic fang	Swordsmanship	-	Explosive circle
Sonic stabbing	Swordsmanship	-	Tearing lightning
Lacerating wave	Swordsmanship	Earth	Infernal torrent
Iron slicer	Swordsmanship	-	Infernal torrent
Flight from the Wyvern	Swordsmanship	(Elevation)	Flight of the Phoenix
Destruction	Swordsmanship	Earth	Tearing lightning
Lightning strike	Swordsmanship	Light (Paralysis - Elevation)	Flight of the phoenix
Rain of swords: alpha	Swordsmanship	-	Tearing lightning
Wind cut	Swordsmanship	Air (Elevation)	Burning Squall
Sovereign slash	Swordsmanship	-	Burning Squall
Double demonic fang	Swordsmanship	-	Burning Squall
Sonic stab 2	Swordsmanship	-	Explosive circle
Eternal devastation	Swordsmanship	Earth	Burning wave
Blades of nothingness	Swordsmanship	-	Burning wave

List of Artes deShionne

Arte	Master Arte	Element & direction	Effect
First Aid	Arte astral	-	Lightly heals an ally's health
Circle of care	Arte astral	-	Gradually restores the HP of allies within the circumference of the circle
Revitalization	Arte astral	-	Restores the health of all allies
Dissipation	Arte astral	-	Heals the physical damage of an ally
Resurrection	Arte astral	-	Heals the physical damage of all allies
Large radius	Pustolet strike	-	Reanimates a knocked-out ally
Water Gemini	Hitting with a gun	Water	-
Lunar explosion	Hitting with a gun	-	-
Lunar Corruption	Hitting with a gun	-	-
Gravity field	Hitting with a gun	Darkness (MAledicti on)	-
Annihilation	Hitting with a gun	Fire	-
Instant cyan (DLC)	Hitting with a gun	Air	-
Ignis Celestra	Explosive strike	Fire	-
Ignis Diffus	Explosive strike	Fire	-
Tonitus Celestra	Explosive strike	Light (Paralysis)	-
Tonitus Pluvia	Explosive strike	Light (Paralysis)	-

Luke Celestra	Explosive strike	Light	-
Luke Divisio	Explosive strike	Light	-
Aranea Celestra	Explosive strike	Light (Paralysis)	-
Aranea Lubes	Explosive strike	Light (Paralysis)	-
Detonation	Hitting with a gun	-	-
Toxicity	Hitting with a gun	Darkness (Poison)	-
Spear Sweep	Hitting with a gun	-	-
Scorched earth	Hitting with a gun	Fire	-
Tres Ventos	Hitting with a gun	Air	-
Aqueous impact	Hitting with a gun	Water (Downhill)	-
Glacio Celestra	Explosive strike	Water (Gel)	-
Glacio Burst	Explosive strike	Water (Gel)	-
Volcanic strike	Arte astral	Fire	-
Flaming tornado	Arte astral	Fire	-
Explosion	Arte astral	Fire	-
Geyser	Arte astral	Water	-
Ice thrower	Arte astral	Water (Gel)	-
Ice Storm (DLC)	Arte astral	Water (Gel)	-
Rayon (DLC)	Arte astral	Light	-

Devouring fire	Hitting with a gun	-	Arte mystique	
Explosive charge	Hitting with a gun	-	Arte mystique	

Rinwell

Arte	Master Arte	Element & direction	Effect
Concentration	Strike of light	-	Increases the power of an ally's strikes by 30%.
Acuity	Strike of light	-	Increases an ally's elemental attack by 30%.
Rafale	Air Strike	Air	-
Photonic lightning	Strike of light	Light	-
Rising water	Water Strike	Water	-
Lightning orb	Strike of light	Light (Paralysis)	-
Thunderfield	Strike of light	Light (Paralysis)	-
Windy whirlwind	Air Strike	Air (Elevation)	-
Moisturizing orb	Water Strike	Water	-
Heavenly Hammer	Strike of light	Light (Paralysis)	-
Sharp cyclone	Air Strike	Air	-
Flight of the swallow	Air Strike	Air	-
Electrical discharge	Strike of light	Light (Paralysis)	-
Cold Trap	Water Strike	Water (Gel)	-

Puddle	Water Strike	Water (Downhill)	-
Volcanic strike	Strike of light	Fire	-
Geyser	Water Strike	Water	-
Ice thrower	Water Strike	Water (Gel)	-
Rising tide	Water Strike	Water	-
Aerial stabbing	Air Strike	Air	-
Crossed blade	Air Strike	Air	-
Cyclone	Air Strike	Air	-
Thunder Blade	Strike of light	Light (Paralysis)	-
Sacred Spear	Strike of light	Light (Paralysis)	-
Divine sword	Strike of light	Light (Paralysis)	-
Maelstrom	Water Strike	Water	-
Shooting star	Strike of light	Light (Paralysis)	-
Stormy weather	Strike of light	-	-
Burst of arrows (DLC)	Water Strike	Water	-
Croc de vent (DLC)	Air Strike	Air	-
Divine Ray (DLC)	Strike of light	Light (Paralysis)	-
Ecstatic divine roar	Strike of light	Light	Arte mystique

Aquarian Damnation	Water Strike	Water	Arte mystique

List of Artes de Dohalim

Arte	Master Arte	Element & direction	Effect
Care	Recovery	-	Restores an ally's health
Healing	Recovery	-	Significantly restores an ally's health
Regeneration	Recovery	-	Gradually restores an ally's HP
Enchanted Circle (DLC)	Recovery	Light	Quickly restores the health of allied people in the circle's circumference
Dissipation	Recovery	-	Heals the physical damage of all allies
Resurrection	Recovery	-	Reanimates a knocked-out ally
Barrier	Recovery	-	Increases the defence and elemental defence of an ally by 30%.
Lionheart	Recovery	-	Increases the JA recovery rate of an ally
Storm	Baton twirling	-	-
Catapult	Baton twirling	-	-
Lonely captivity	Baton twirling	Earth	-
Penumbra	Baton twirling	Earth (Elevation)	-

Elusive deity	Baton twirling	Darkness (Curse - Rise)	-
Seismic failure	Baton twirling	Earth	-
Crescent lightning	Baton twirling	Air	-
Bloody flowers	Baton twirling	Darkness (Curse)	-
Raging Luna Storm (DLC)	Baton twirling	Air	-
Rotary hammer	Baton twirling	-	-
Tornado surge	Baton twirling	- (Downhill)	-
Sonic Lance	Baton twirling	-	-
Demon's spear	Baton twirling	Darkness (Curse)	-
Rising wave	Baton twirling	Earth	-
Eagle rage	Baton twirling		-
Stalagmite	Demonic Strike	Earth	-
Gravisphere	Demonic Strike	Earth	-
Land Elk	Demonic Strike	Earth	-
Negative portal	Demonic Strike	Darkness (Curse)	-
Bloody howl	Demonic Strike	Darkness (Curse)	-
Execution	Demonic Strike	Darkness (Curse)	-
Water Snake (DLC)	Demonic Strike	Water	-

Tectonic fission	Demonic Strike	-	Arte mystique
Break in time	Demonic Strike	Darkness (Curse)	Arte mystique

List of Artes de Law

Arte	Master Arte	Element & direction	Effect
Greenhouse storm	Punching	-	-
Fangs	Punching	-	-
Dragon Throwing	Leg strike	- (Elevation)	-
Lightning tornado	Leg strike	Air	-
Techtonic punch	Fist strike	Earth	-
Grazing flame	Leg strike	Fire	-
Dance of the swallow	Leg strike	- (Elevation)	-
Lightning Mirage	Punching	-	-
Inspiration	Spirit	-	Restores some PV to Law

Arte	Master Arte	Element & direction	Effect
Steel	Spirit	-	Increases Law's attack and elementary attack by 30%.
Super swallow dance	Leg strike	-	-
Greenhouse hurricane	Punching	- (Elevation)	-
Divine fang	Punching	-	-
Snake Fist (DLC)	Punching	Water (Elevation)	-
Dark Wind (DLC)	Leg strike	Air	-
Sparkling wild roar (DLC)	Punching	Light (Paralysis)	-
Eagle Loon	Leg strike	- (Downhill)	-
Sparkling Dragon	Leg strike	Air	-
Inferno punch	Punching	Fire	-
Bolero of fangs	Leg strike	-	-
Hegemonic flare-up	Punching	Fire -(Descending)	-
Eagle Assault	Leg strike	- (Downhill)	-
A deadly chain of events	Leg strike	- (Downhill)	-
Dark claw of thunder	Leg strike	Light (Paralysis)	Arte mystique
Scarlet skies	Leg strike	Fire	Arte mystique

List of Artes de Kisara

Arte	Master Arte	Element & direction	Effect
Protective aura	Shield strike	Light	Heals an ally

Roar of the lion	Shield strike	-	Reinforced in case of custody
Burning meteors	Powerful strike	-	-
Incendiary emission	Powerful strike	Earth	-
Tiger Blade	Shield strike	-	Reinforced in case of custody
Piercing roar	Shield strike	Light (Paralysis)	Reinforced in case of custody
Rolling Thunder	Shield strike	Earth	Reinforced in case of custody
Hurricane slice	Powerful strike	Air (Elevation)	-
Crescent moon	Shield strike	Earth	Reinforced in case of custody
Wyvern Storm	Shield strike	Air	Reinforced in case of custody
Crossfire	Powerful strike	Fire	-
Maximum explosion	Shield strike	Earth	Reinforced in case of custody
Slag attack	Shield strike	Earth	Reinforced in case of custody
Lunar Arc	Powerful strike	Earth	-
Ice bonfire	Shield strike	Water (Gel)	Reinforced in case of custody
Sadistic descent	Shield strike	- (Elevation)	-
Water snake furrow (DLC)	Shield strike	Water	Reinforced in case of custody
Descending Storm (DLC)	Shield strike	Air	Reinforced in case of custody
Dazzling Spin (DLC)	Shield strike	Light	Reinforced in case of custody
Series of lightning bolts	Powerful strike	Air (Downhill)	-

Assault of the beast	Shield strike	-	-
Chaos stabbing	Powerful strike	-	-
Lance of light	Shield strike	-	-
Tearing storm	Shield strike	Air (descent)	-
Blizzard Flower	Shield strike	Water (Freezing - Descending)	-
Fire demolisher	Shield strike	-	Arte mystique
Last hope	Shield strike	-	Arte mystique

Combinations to obtain Rinwell's Special Artes

As a reminder, to load a spell with Rinwell, first hold the Arte button to delay the casting of the spell, then R1 to store it. You can store as many spells as you want. When only the spell element is specified, just use a beginning Arte to load it faster because using a more powerful spell does not increase the power anyway. Be careful, the order is important!

METEOR STORM

Meteor Storms is obtained by charging Volcanic Strike once, then 3 lightning spells.

MAELSTRÖM

Maelstrom is obtained by charging 2 water spells and 2 air spells.

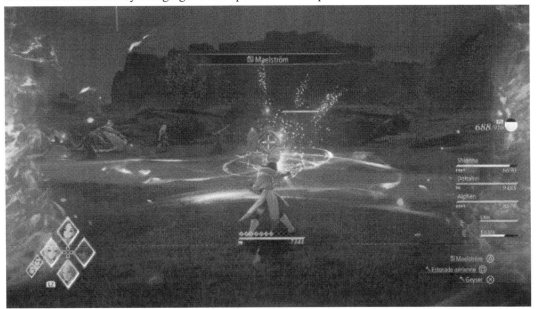

FLAMING TORNADO AND EXPLOSION

Flaming Tornado and Explosion follow the classic rule, i.e. two fire spells for Flaming Tornado, and three fire spells for Explosion. However, you can't learn these spells directly, so you'll have to go through the combinations each time.

SHOOTING STAR

Spinning Star is obtained by combining two water spells and Holy Lance.

TIDAL WAVE, DIVINE SWORD AND CYCLONE

Tidal Wave, Divine Sword and Cyclone are obtained by combining 3 water spells, 3 light spells and 3 air spells respectively.

Main adventure

Kingdom of Calaglia

MOSGUL

You start the game in the prison camp. For now, just go to the doctor in front of you. Once you've been treated, go back to your bed in the north. The next day, go to your workstation to trigger a cinematic

ZIONNE MINE TUNNEL

Once you are back in control of the main character, visit Shionne in the dungeon to the north. After the cinematic, you'll finally get some action: continue north to exit the mine. On the way, a guard in armour blocks your path and you are launched into your first fight. Familiarise yourself with the various attack and dodge options. If this is your first Tales of, you should know that in addition to regular attacks, you can also use Artes: these are much more powerful attacks than regular attacks and will make your combos much more effective. You can consult the Arte menu to have details on each of your available Artes.

After the fight, continue on your way. On the left, in the cell, you will find an apple jelly to heal yourself in case of emergency. A little further on you will meet a soldier and a wolf. As you've noticed, you can't die at the moment so take the opportunity to test everything you can. A little further on, you'll have a third fight with Shionne this time.

The latter will accompany you to the mine exit. You will also unlock your first skit: don't hesitate to look regularly at the bottom right of the screen. If R1 appears, it means that a skit is available. Be aware that there is a trophy/achievement "Moulin à paroles" for having seen more than 300 of them, so take the time to watch them (you can also skip them, what counts is to trigger them). Then continue to the mine exit.

After long cinematics, Shionne officially joins the team. You can now die and you unlock Healing

Points (HP): these points allow you to use Shionne's healing arts. Feel free to go to the Strategy menu to tell her how to use her healing spells more effectively. When you are ready, continue and leave the mine.

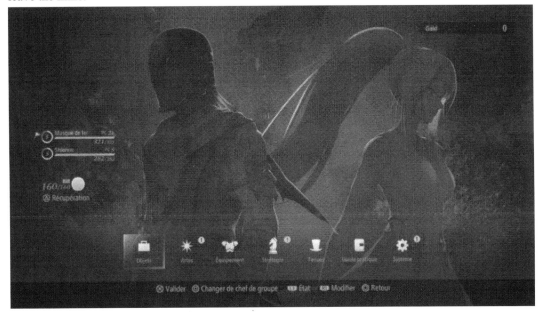

SANDINUS RAVINE

In this new area, exploration is still rather limited at the moment. You will encounter three wolves on your way. They shouldn't be too much of a problem. However, the golem that comes next can be a bit more intimidating. Don't be afraid: if he does hit hard, you can easily beat him if you hit the big orange core on his back which is his weak point. Looking for ways to break the cores and exploit the enemies' weaknesses is a good reflex to have as soon as possible.

To the right of the golem, you will find a chest with three Resurrection Vials. Then continue until you find a place to camp. Camping is very important to be able to fill up your SPs and to cook (mechanics that will be introduced later). Once the camping is over, go back to your route and collect as many resources as possible (rocks, plants...). These resources reappear after a while and are marked on your map, which makes them very easy to find when you need them. There are also vines on the left side of the wooden bridge leading to a lake. On the other side you will find Sage, which can increase a character's health bar by 50 HP.

On your way, the game will draw attention to your first Giant Zeugle: ignore it for now, it's probably not a good idea to try and fight it now (it's level 43). A little further to the right, perched on a tree, you will find your first Dahna Owl: this will give you the Dog Tail accessory. Continue on your way to the gate. When there is an owl nearby, you will hear some kind of loud "Hou - hou", so don't hesitate to look for them when you hear them (you will get the trophies / successes "Owl lover" and "Ornithologist" for having found respectively 13 and 32 owls, as well as a last trophy for having found all 38 owls)

ULZEBEK

When you get to Ulzebek, go to the Red Crows' hideout at the top of the stairs. After receiving your new outfit, go and talk to Nayth right next to the well. You will then be introduced to the game's side quests. If you can continue straight into the main adventure, in addition to the basic rewards, doing this quest could get you your first title and unlock the skill panel, so it may be worth taking five minutes to do. Then go back and talk to Nayth in the house.

Before leaving for the ruins of Fagan, you may have heard an owl when you were in the house. Climb the ladder inside and then onto the roof: owl number 2 is on the drying rack. This one gives you Rabbit Ears.

ARID LANDS OF IGLIA

As soon as you arrive, a tutorial about bonus attacks starts: bonus attacks are very important not only to inflict "free" extra damage, but especially to benefit from the unique advantages of each character. For example, Shionne's attack stuns flying enemies. So remember to use them when the time is right.

For the rest of the area, you can explore at your leisure up to the ruins. In the rest of this guide, we will only cover the location of important collectibles in the open-world areas (owls, chests...). At the entrance to the area, climb the creepers to find a chest containing 500 Gald. In the small alley to the right of the ruins' entrance, you will also find Lavender, increasing a character's Strength by 5. The ladder to the southwest of the map leads to Hinou #3, which gives you the Spotted Cat's Ears.

Before entering the ruins, you will unlock the ability to cook while camping. Cooking is of utmost importance because of the stats boosts it provides. In general, try to always have an active dish, especially during boss fights. After cooking for the first time with Shionne, you will unlock his "Instant Cooking" title. Then you just have to enter the ruins.

FAGAN RUINS

To get through the red portal, simply activate the control panel next to it. Once through the entrance, head right to find a chest at the far end containing two Resurrection Vials, then take the path to the left, and climb the stairs to the top floor.

On level 2 you will find a chest in the rectangular area to the south containing an Apple Jelly. Then go west and jump across the street, then enter the room on the right to find a Chamomile (increases a character's concentration). Turn around and go east to level 3.

Before activating the green device, search the two rooms to the west: you'll find an Orange Jelly in the first one, and a device to deactivate the lasers blocking access to a room on level 2. Return to this room to find a Piercing Emblem, which is probably your first accessory. You can then go back up to activate the green device and continue.

After obtaining Shionne's new outfit (and the Noble Rose weapon), you can leave the dungeon and return to Ulzebek. You then finally unlock the ability to do the quick trips once you are out. Back in Ulzebek, you learn that your opponents are slaughtering innocent people. So you return to Mosgul.

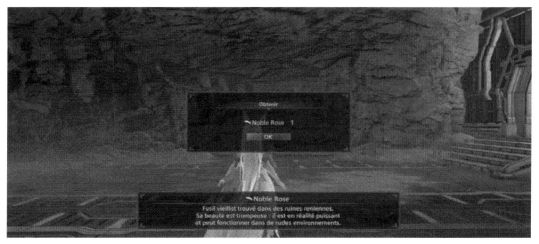

KYRD GARRISON AND RETURN TO MOSGUL

Regarding the important collectibles in this area, in the isolated area in the centre you will find a chest with Meat Remains and another with 500 Gald. In the area a little further south you will find the recipe for 'Roasted Mushrooms'. In the outlying area north of the entrance to Mosgul you will find Verbena. For the moment, you can't do anything else in the area so go back to Mosgul.

As soon as you arrive, a fight against an armoured guard starts. Move forward a little until you hear the Doc: go help him and beat the armoured soldier.

FLAME TRENCH

If you take the first right, in the house on the left, you will find the owl giving the Dog Ears. Then go straight on to the next area. Here, just past the castle gate on the left, you will find a small off-centre area with Saffron (increases elemental defence by 5).

Just opposite is another owl giving the left bandage. Then continue west as you can't go east anyway. On your way you will find a house with a locked door so ignore it for now and use the creepers a little further down, then continue straight on

BALSEPH CASTLE

When you arrive in the castle, Iron Mask unlocks the title 'The Fiery Sword', and its bonus attack gets a boost by allowing you to take down all enemies, the power of which is directly dependent on the amount of HP you sacrifice, and deals even more damage if the enemy is down. You will have to complete a tutorial right afterwards teaching you how to use Fiery Slice. To keep it simple, you simply press and hold one of the three Artes keys, then release to use Fiery Slice. You also unlock the ability to perform Bonus Strikes, a sort of ultimate move that unlocks depending on your combo and the opponent's HP (the blue diamond-shaped gauge on the enemies).

Right after the battle, the game will also introduce you to field actions: you can unlock new passages in exchange for Healing Points. Use 8 healing points to stop the fire in front of you. You then have the choice to either run straight ahead or go around and sacrifice HP to remove the wall of fire (there is a mineral source just in front of the wall). To the west, you will see a lift but you can't use it at the moment so continue straight ahead.

On the second level, sacrifice 16 SP to get behind the wall of flames and find a Bone Shard Armour. Sacrifice another 16 SP to find a Warrior's Emblem this time. You can then continue on to the next level.

When you arrive, you will notice a soldier attacking a child. After the fight, you get the key to the lift. Shionne also gets the title "A Woman with a Grip", which gives you access to her strong point of holding down your Artes keys when using grenades to make them much more powerful. Remember that you have to reload before you can use this strength if you run out of grenades. In the side rooms you will find three Orange Jellies, some leftover meat, a chest with two Resurrection

Vials, and a Jasmine (increases Stamina by 5). You will also find the owl giving the Rabbit's Tail among the chickens in the central west room

The key to progressing through the dungeon is in the centre-east room, protected by two soldiers and a wolf, in the left-hand room on the cupboard. You can then use the lift to progress between the different levels of the castle.

On the 4th floor, you will find the first giant Zeugle that you can actually defeat: the 'Poison Armadillo'. These enemies may seem impressive, but don't be afraid to fight them because as a reward you can get Astral Flowers, an item that increases your SP by 10. You can click here for more details on the fight itself (strategy, video of the fight...) and on all the other Giant Zeugles.

Also on the 4th floor, you will find a chest with 2 Astral Crystal Grains. To the north, you can sacrifice 18 SP to obtain the Garnet accessory, which reduces fire and water damage by 50%, which can be used directly in the fight that follows. All you have to do then is beat the two guards in front of the other lift and use the beast key to access the last level. Save yourself as your first boss fight, Lord Balseph, awaits you.

Boss: Lord Balseph

Balseph's attacks are fire elemental attacks. In the Castle, on the top floor, you can find the Garnet accessory that reduces fire damage by 50%, which will help you greatly in this fight. Give this accessory to the main character instead, as he is the only one who will actually be in contact with the boss.

As for Shionne, it is better to leave her to the AI to take care of her. In the strategies, make sure to include an action with the following variables: "Always", "Stay away from enemies" and "No restrictions" so that she stays as far away from Balseph as possible. For these artes, only let her heal artes and the artes with the elemental affinity Water be activated if you already have them, and couple them with an accessory that increases water damage (otherwise, leave her other attacks activated). Don't hesitate to go to the blacksmith to improve an accessory and improve the damage of the Water attacks.

As for the fight itself, Balseph hits very hard but is very slow. The easiest way to defeat him is to let him finish his combos (which never exceed three consecutive attacks) and then link them with your Artes. If you feel comfortable with perfect dodges, his axe strikes are very phoned in and therefore a simple source of damage. Even if you don't feel like you're attacking her often, Shionne will probably do most of the work from a distance with her Artes. You are only there as a distraction.

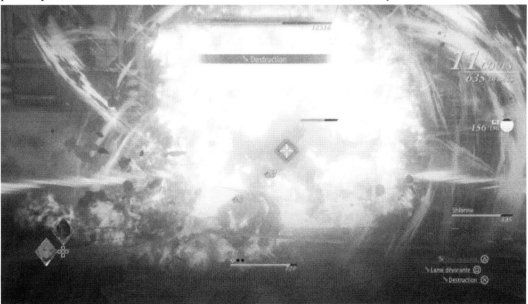

During the first phase of combat, the game will introduce special bonus strikes that are only available against certain bosses. When Balseph is in the air to attack, press the directional pad to launch the attack and knock him down.

Once Balseph has lost half his life, the second phase of the fight begins. While Balseph himself has more or less the same attacks, it is the appearance of the giant monster behind him that is the problem. Pay attention to what Shionne says and warns you when he is about to attack so that you can prepare yourself to avoid his attacks.

When Balseph enters Out of Bounds, he can launch his Mystic Arte. If this is the case, this is your chance to lash out for a couple of dozen seconds as his Mystic Arte is prepared. However, be careful not to be too greedy so that you can avoid it when the attack is launched (if you haven't killed it before).

Kingdom of Cyslodia

THE GATES OF FIRE: MEETING WITH RINWELL

When you wake up in Ulzebek, Alphen gets the title 'Emissary of Liberation'. Two side quests are now available in Ulzebek if you want to take a break. Otherwise, continue on to the fire gates. On the way, you will unlock the Shionne's Field action, which involves sacrificing SPs to heal the sick in exchange for rewards. Then take the lift back to Kyrd's Garrison to access the gates.

After meeting a mysterious girl, she will faint, so you decide to return to Ulzebek so she can rest. Head back to Mosgul to talk to the Doc and get some medicine (you can use the quick trip). He advises you to go to the Kyrd Garrison. The medicine is in the central area, on a shelf. Then go back to the Doc in Mosgul to make sure you've taken the right thing, then Tilsa in Ulzebek. Once the cinematics are over, Zephyr joins the group and you head off to the Cliffs of Lacerda.

LACERDA CLIFFS

At the very south end of the cliff overlooking the castle you will find 1 Saffron. Just below is also a chest containing 1 Resurrection Vial. If you approach the small eastern area, a cinematic with Hootle and then a fight will start. Finally, just in front of the camp, you will find an owl giving the Mounted Glasses.

ULVHAN CAVE

The beginning of the cave is very bossy, but it is an opportunity to discover new types of Zeugles, notably the Montitentacles and the Deceptive Effigies. These two enemies are both weak to wind, so don't hesitate to use Alphen's Cutting Wind. Also be sure to have Shionne's Restoration activated as you will be poisoned quite often. To progress, continue straight ahead and climb the ladder.

At the intersection you have the choice of going straight on or turning right. The right-hand path is the 'right way' out of the dungeon, so we'll keep going straight for now. On the way, behind three Montitentacles, there is a chest with 3 Vials of Panacea.

At the very end of this path is a giant Zeugle: the Tumultuous Montitacule. This level 15 Zeugle is weak to wind and resists earth attacks. Its weak point is behind its head and will be accompanied by two classic Montitentacles. If you want more details on how to defeat it, you can click here. Defeating it will net you an astral flower, as well as access to the chest containing the Onyx Boot armour. You can then return to the normal path. A little further on you will find 1 Chamomile protected by a Deceptive Effigy. You will then just have to leave the dungeon.

SILVER PLAINS

Once in the area, don't hesitate to rush to the campfire to restore your PS. When you get close, a cinematic will start. You will then unlock the possibility of creating accessories thanks to the Goldsmith. The Goldsmith is essential to be able to create overpowered accessories, in any case much more than those you find in chests. You can click here if you want a more detailed guide to goldsmithing. Finally, you also get the recipe for 'Vegetable Soup'.

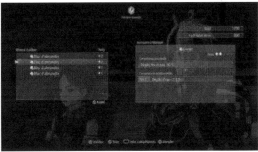

As far as the area is concerned, you can imagine that the enemies are weak to the Artes de Feu, which will be to Shionne's advantage, but also to Alphen's Tranchant ardent. For collectibles, you will find a chest containing 850 Gald in the isolated area to the north. To the far east, some vines will lead you to a chest with 1 Vial of Resurrection. Finally, just before you leave the area, an owl is just over the bridge and gives you the left eye patch.

MESSIA 224

As soon as you get home, you meet Law, who starts a fight with you: the best thing to do is to ignore him completely and concentrate on the soldiers and the wolf. When they are eliminated, the fight ends and a cinematic begins.

Once the cinematic is over, you unlock the "Vegetable Juice" recipe, Rinwell joins the team, and you unlock Hootle who will help you find the owls (later). Return to Messia 224 to find out what happened to Zephyr. Right in front of you is a side quest asking you to kill 7 ice wolves: it's up to you whether you want to take the time to do it or not. Two other side quests are also available in the village at the moment. To the west, behind an ox and hidden in a basket is an owl with wolf ears. When you are done with the side activities, go up to the top, cross the bridge and talk to the citizens. You are now on your way to Cysloden.

RUDHIR FOREST

Exploring the forest is fairly straightforward: you'll find a chest to the west near the lake containing 1050 Gald, and another chest containing an Onyx Robe when you cross the lake. Nearby, climb the vines to find a person to heal with Shionne: you will get 2 Earth Seeds. In the far eastern area, you will find 1 Verbena. At the very end of the forest, a local warns you that a huge wolf is blocking the way. Prepare yourself well, because a boss fight is waiting for you.

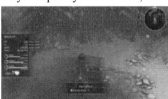

BOSS: LEADER OF THE ICE PACK

Leader of the wolf pack 16 Fire 12 - 14 depending on the chosen difficulty

The leader of the ice pack is, as you might expect, weak in firearms. Fortunately, you have Shionne and Alphen to exploit this weakness. Leave only the Healing and Fire Artes activated on Shionne to make sure she only exploits the fire weakness (if you don't control her).

You then have the choice of playing with Alphen or Rinwell: both are very good choices. If you play with Alphen, make sure you use his Strength to sacrifice HP for more power as often as possible. With the pack leader's fire weakness, your hits will do huge damage.

Playing with Rinwell for this fight is also a very good idea as she is particularly strong at the beginning of the game. Indeed, thanks to her strength, she can have access to endgame spells right away. While she doesn't have access to fire skills, the Divine Sword spell is particularly effective for this fight. At this stage of the game, your only way to cast Divine Sword is to charge two Light spells, then cast a third (it doesn't matter what the rank is, so you might as well take the weakest spells so you can charge them as quickly as possible).

With Divine Sabre, not only can you quickly get rid of the other wolves, but the attack covers such a large area that the boss can't avoid it. Be careful though, the AI will have a hard time keeping aggro and it's not uncommon for the boss to only focus on you at times.

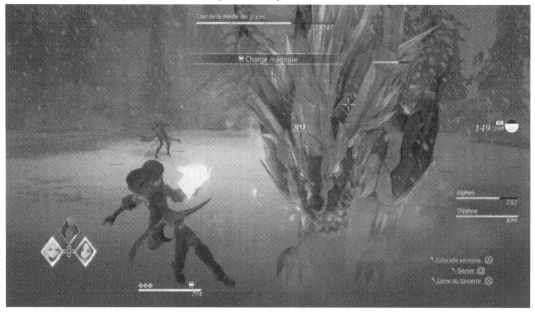

NEVIRA SNOW PLAINS & THE OWL FOREST

Once you arrive, take advantage of the camp to recover your SPs after the fight against the leader of the pack. Just after, Hootle will draw your attention to a path on the right and the quest "The Owl Forest" will start. Examine the owl to be teleported to the owl forest. Approach the two owls on the tree trunk to make the owl king leave. You then get the Black Battle Suit, and the title "Friend of the Birds" for Rinwell. With the cinematic, you understand that you will get rewards according to the number of owls found. There are 38 in all to find to complete this quest.

After collecting all your rewards, return to the snowy plains. To enter the town, you will need to use the secret passage, which is the northernmost entrance on the map. Before entering, take the time to explore the area a little: you will find 1 Sage in the northwest and a chest containing an Emblem of Courage in a chest next to it requiring you to sacrifice 21 SP. In the middle of the lake is also an owl giving a Wolf's Tail. When you have finished, enter the secret passage to enter the town.

CYSLODEN

Once in Cysloden, go straight on to find the base of the Silver Swords. As you pass, you will find an owl giving out Sunglasses just above the water source

After meeting Menek, Rinwell unlocks the title "Silver Swords". Then leave the house, go up the stairs, and continue to the central square avenue. Then take the first right to progress the plot. After meeting Law, return to Menek at the Silver Swords Hideout.

UNDERGROUND CANAL

Once in the Underground Canal, a tutorial on Rinwell's bonus attack starts: if you use it when an enemy charges an Astral Arte, you can steal this spell and use it yourself. On top of that, the enemy will be knocked down, making it a formidable weapon when the situation calls for it.

You can then start exploring the Canal: you will find a chest guarded by Montitentacules containing 1300 Gald in the southernmost room. In the south-west, you will find a person who can be healed by Shionne for 21 SP. In exchange you will get 2 strange mega cores. Just after you will find a chest guarded by muddy blobs containing an Onyx Cape. In the central rectangular room, jump from the right to a chest containing 1 cure. Just below it you will find 1 Jasmine. Once you are at the Healing Light level, save and prepare for battle.

BOSS: HIVE OF SLIMY BLOB

Muddy blob hive 17 Fire 14 - 16 depending on the chosen difficulty

Like the leader of the wolf pack, this boss is weak to fire attacks. The same strategy can therefore be used to defeat him, i.e. let only the Healing and Fire Artes be activated on Shionne, and play with Alphen or Rinwell, the former to exploit the fire weakness thanks to her strength, the latter to use endgame spells (also thanks to her strength).

The first part of the fight is fairly straightforward, try to hit the inside of the mouth as this is where the boss' core is, but don't stand in the middle of it to avoid the risk of being attacked too often.

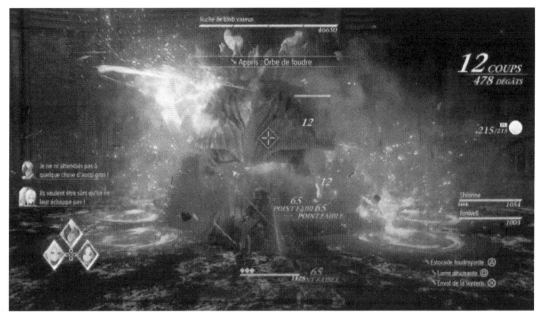

The problems start especially with the second phase. Throughout the rest of the fight, the boss can summon loads of blobs to help him during the fight, ad infinitum (the number of blobs summoned seems to vary depending on the difficulty chosen). In fact, there's no point in wasting your time trying to kill them all, focus on the boss instead. However, make sure you never waste Rinwell's Bonus Strike and only use it when many blobs and/or the boss are about to cast a spell to avoid too much pressure at once.

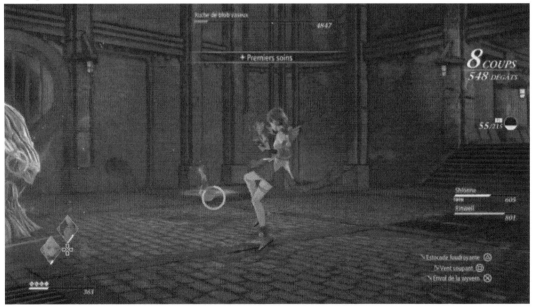

Another very problematic element during this fight is the poison. Indeed, the blobs will put puddles of poison everywhere on the field, so much so that it will quickly become difficult to avoid being poisoned. To avoid all this, make sure you create three accessories that give you immunity to poison and put one on each character. This will make it easier for you to attack the boss as you don't have to worry about avoiding the poison that is almost everywhere in the arena.

Once the fight is over, you can leave the canal and go to a safe hiding place. You will then learn that Zephyr's execution will take place soon. Use the inn to get your SPs and cook, then head towards the avenue of the fountain square, then the central square. On your way, you will have to fight three soldiers. After the fight, a cinematic will start. A second fight starts, and for the first time you unlock the possibility for your characters to enter the Off-Limits mode. During this time, you can use your Artes without consuming JA, nor risk being interrupted by an enemy attack. In addition to this, you can cast a Mystic Arte by pressing two Arte buttons in Out of Bounds. Since using a Mystic Arte ends the Out of Bounds, wait until the bar is almost empty to make one.

Once the fight is over, return to the hideout. Law then officially joins the team. His strong point is that he can break the guards of shielded enemies. Moreover, the more you manage to attack without being hit, the more powerful his attacks become. Then head for the Prison Tower via the central square. Be aware that if you decide to explore the city, enemies may attack you.

Just before you enter the tower, a tutorial about Law's bonus attack starts. To complete the tutorial, you only need to use Law's bonus attack twice to destroy the shields.

RIVILLE PRISON TOWER

At the moment, you can only examine the elevator, as all other doors are closed. Bad luck, the elevator is also closed. The door to the east, on the other hand, is open. Here you can sacrifice 11 SP to break the wall with Law. In the northeast room, sacrifice 23 SP to find a chest containing 1 Alexandrite. In the southwestern room, you will find a lone soldier: he is in fact an undercover agent informing you that there is a way to infiltrate the office opposite. Go there and examine the horse statue. It is the key to the collection room.

Return to the previous room and go up the stairs to use the key. Beat the guards and continue straight on. Go up to the desk and examine the book. You will find a button you can press. Go back to the entrance room, beat the guards, and enter the room to the north.

In this new area, go straight ahead: you'll notice a giant Zeugle locked in a cage on the left, but you don't have the key to do anything about it at the moment (it's a side quest that unlocks later). Further on, you will find a chest with a dead body right in front of it. The moment you open the chest, the four statues around it will attack you. The chest contains 1 Vial of Resurrection. You will find 1 Sage right next to it. Opposite, you will find an office guarded by wolves. Beat them and get the Elevator Key level 1. Go back to the lift and go to the next level.

On level 2 go straight on until you find a new lift for which you also need a key. To the northwest you will find a chest with 1 Vial of Panacea. Behind the wall requiring 23 SP to pass located in the north centre, you will find a chest containing 1 Sailor's Gown. To the north-east, the chest contains 1500 Gald. Behind the second wall requiring 23 SP to pass in the centre of the area, you will find the Haute Couture armour.

Eventually you will find a room guarded by several soldiers, a wolf and a red soldier. Behind it is the control panel for the lift. In the room to the south you will find an owl on the left perched on the cupboard: it gives you the Devil's Horns. You will also find a chest with 1 Remedy. You can now turn around and go to level 3, but you will have to beat another red guard before doing so. Once on level 3, heal yourself and save because the fight against the boss of the chapter, Lord Ganabelt Valkyris awaits you.

Boss : Lord Ganabelt Valkyris

Lord Ganabelt Valkyris 19 - 17 - 19 depending on the chosen difficulty

For this fight, it will be very important to keep Law's and Rinwell's bonus hits to be able to use them when needed. Ganabelt has no particular weaknesses so you can use the Artes you like best. That being said, Rinwell's Tidal Wave spell works particularly well for this fight as it will do damage to both the real Ganabelt and all of his clones. At this point in the game, your only way to access Rising Tide is to store two water abilities, then cast a third. To avoid having to do this manually, only let the (magical, avoid physical) water artes activate on Rinwell and the AI will be smart enough to do the rest of the work.

It is also advisable to play with a more physically oriented character (Law and Alphen) to keep Ganabelt's attention and allow Shionne and Rinwell to use their spells safely. On the higher difficulties, it may be better to play with Law as at this stage of the game he dies very easily and the AI is not competent enough to dodge enough hits to survive.

You will notice very quickly that Ganabelt is permanently surrounded by some sort of shield which greatly reduces the damage inflicted. In fact, as soon as you can, use Law's Bonus Strike to remove this barrier and start doing real damage. Breaking the barrier will put Ganabelt down for a long time,so it's the perfect time to use Alphen's strong point and sacrifice as many HP as possible to do massive damage.

When Ganabelt comes to his senses, he will start summoning clones of himself. Eliminate the clones first or you won't make it! In particular, try to use Rinwell's Bonus Strike as soon as several clones are about to cast spells to stop them. Alphen's Bonus Strike also works, but will only work on one clone at a time unless you can group them together and hit several at once. If you use the above technique with Rinwell to gain access to advanced spells now (such as Tidal Wave, Divine Sword or Cyclone), you should be able to eliminate them quickly as long as you are able to act as a distraction.

After losing half his life, Ganabelt will go Off-Limits, summon three clones again, and prepare to launch his Mystic Arte. The goal here will be to kill as many clones as possible so that the attack does less damage (on the highest difficulty, if you don't kill any clones, it will probably be a one-shot on the whole team). Since the clones are harmless during the preparation phase, take control of Alphen and use his strength to bombard them with hits. Don't hesitate to use items to recover life very quickly and to be able to sacrifice some again. With this method, if you can't kill the three clones, you should be able to kill two of them, which makes the Mystic Arte much less dangerous. The rest of the fight is more or less the same as the first phase so you just have to repeat until he dies.

If you are really struggling against this boss, don't hesitate to make the "Alexandrite" accessory which reduces light damage by 50%.

After the battle, head north to the Kingdom of Menancia

FROZEN VALLEY

In the area below the vines to the west you will find 1 Rosemary. At the bottom of the ones further down is a wall of ice to melt for 23 SP to find a Mage's Cloak. On the tree next to the wooden bridge there is an owl giving you the Half-rounders and a person to heal for Shionne giving 5 strawberries. Still in front of the bridge you will find a person on the ground with a side quest allowing you to get the recipe for Apple Pies in exchange for some apples and wheat. You can then camp and move on to the next area.

SAFAR SEA CAVE

After collecting all the ores on the upper level, jump into the hole without the ladder and then jump onto the rock opposite to find a chest containing 1 Vial of Resurrection. Once in the water, start by exploring the northern part, and open the chest protected by four Bugs to find 1800 Gald. On the main beach, climb the first set of stairs, then jump onto the platform just behind to find 1 Cure.

Then jump into the southernmost hole to land on the lower level. In the southernmost room you will find 1 Carapace Pourpoint (beware, the Effigies around will attack you). Just behind the ladder to the top you will find 1 Lavender. Then go up the ladder and jump through the other hole. Here you will find an underwater passage leading to a 1 Ring of Speed. You can then climb back up and exit the cave.

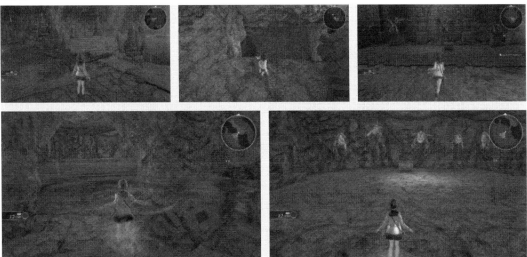

OBSERVATION CENTRE

In the far north you will find 1 Verbena protected by four Bugs. Then, on the way, the side quest "The Healer and her patients" starts automatically. You have a campfire right next to it so don't be afraid to use your SPs to heal them. The first one will give you 2 Beast Tails, and the second one 5 eggs. The poet then appears a little further on and gives you 2 Mollusc Tentacles to complete the quest. At the very south of the area you will find an owl near the fishing bridge giving you the Red Tropical Pin. You can then move on to the next area.

TRASLIDA ROAD

In this zone, after having made a first fight, you will unlock the possibility of obtaining bonuses according to the number of fights that you chain. These bonuses concern EXP, loot, and PC gained so don't hesitate to fight all the enemies on your way. Law also earns the title "The Rebirth of the Silver Wolf". Be careful though, if you manage to max out the gauge and do another fight from behind (only in this area), the Giant Zeugle Great Dragon will come crashing into the fight, so it's at your own risk.

As for collectibles, you will find a person to heal with Shionne under the bridge in the center of the area, and will receive 4 Carp in exchange. If you continue swimming south, you will find a small cave with 1 Sage. On the other side of the river, heading north, there is a chest with 2 Granite Fangs.

On the road to town you will find a man lying on the ground. Talking to him will trigger the side quest to the Ranch. The Ranch is very useful for farming food, and therefore for your cooking, so don't neglect it. You also unlock the title "The Nanny" for Law. When you leave the Ranch, go to the wheat fields, near the horses, to find an owl giving the Demon Wings.

TIETAL PLAINS

Before entering the city, make a diversion to the Plains of Tietal, which can be reached from the very north of the Traslida road. In the south-eastern part, you will find a person to heal with Shionne who will give you 10 Tomatoes in exchange. In the same place, perched on the bridge behind you is an owl giving you the Smiling Glasses. Finally, to the northwest you will find 1 Verbena. You can now return to the Traslida Road to enter the town.

VISCINT

Once in the city, talk to the various villagers indicated on your map. On your way, a scene mentioning the training ground and the side quest "Ground for all, all to the ground" will be triggered. You just have to go to the scene to complete the quest. Nearby where the scene ends is an owl near the vendor right behind you. The owl gives you an Aureole. Once you've talked to all the locals, head to the north exit to explore the quarry where the Dahnians work.

There is nothing interesting at the moment in the mining site 1 so continue straight on. Kisara then comes to meet you, and mentions that Dohalim wants to meet Alphen in his palace just east of Viscint. After the cinematic, Shionne unlocks the title "Trigger Crazy". Finally, return to the entrance square so you can leave the palace and sleep at the Viscint Inn. When you wake up, follow the black cat into the woods.

GILANNE WOOD

Once in the woods, continue straight ahead to chase the black cat. On the outer level, go to the ladder on the south side to reach the middle level. There you will find a chest containing 1 topaz cape. On the eastern side of the outer level you will also find a chest containing 2000 Gald. Then use the middle ladder to go to the inner level.

To the west of the inner level you will find 1 Lavender and to the north-east, lower part in a chest, 1 Opal. That's it for the important collectibles, you just have to continue to the healing circle, and save before the boss fight.

BOSS : ZACARANIA

Boss Zacarania\ Level 23\ Weakness Air\ Recommended 19 – 21

The fight against Zacarania is quite particular: indeed, you will first have to kill its tentacles before being able to hurt it directly. If you try to attack its central part, you will not do any damage (for the moment). Each tentacle has its own life bar, and the main boss' life bar only drops when a tentacle is killed.

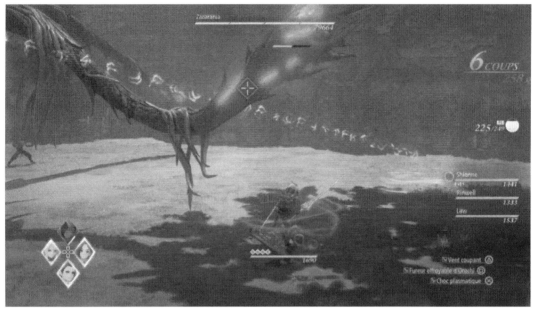

Since Zacarania (and therefore her tentacles) is weak to air, only leave the wind spells activated on Rinwell to push the AI to use Cyclone and do huge damage on several tentacles at once (you can also play her directly). If you decide to play with Alphen, make sure to include at least one Air Arte in your combo. For example, Cutting Wind is not only Air, but also allows you to be in the air afterwards, which will allow you to continue your combo in the air, and thus reach the tentacles that are much harder to hit on the ground. When they are on the ground on the other hand, use Orochi's Frightful Fury to do massive damage to the tentacle.

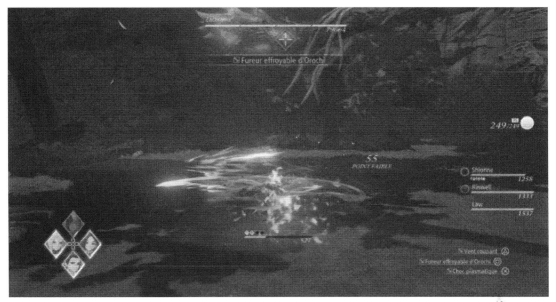

In the middle of the fight, three Montitentacles will appear: eliminate them as quickly as possible to avoid the situation getting out of hand. Once again, accessories that make you immune to poison will come in very handy as it will be difficult to dodge all the attacks between the boss and the mobs.

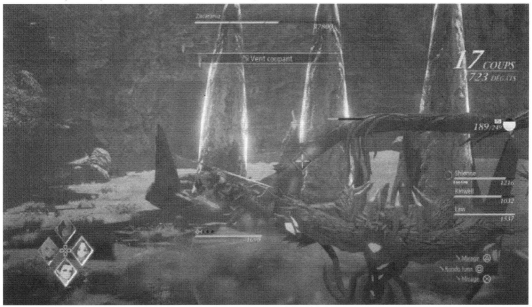

Once all the tentacles are destroyed, you can finally attack the central body. You've done the later, Zacarania can't really defend itself now so finish it.

After the fight, use the camp to collect your SP and cook, then enter the next dungeon.

BOSS: CAPTAIN KISARA OF THE GUARD

Captain Kisara of the Guard level 23 Recommended 20 - 21

Kisara has a huge amount of HP and an equally impressive defence. Fortunately, you only need to remove half of them to get through the fight. Whenever you get the chance, use Law's Bonus Strike to break her guard and take her down. Then, use Alphen's strong point and sacrifice as many HP as possible to do huge damage. Kisara is very slow so you shouldn't have much trouble dodging her attacks, just don't be too aggressive and the fight should go well.

After the fight, you have the possibility to spend the night there. Before doing so, go and open the chest opposite to get 1 cure. After a well-deserved rest, return to Viscint with the fast trip. There you will be given a Bracelet to give to Kisara at the Palace, then return to the Viscint Inn. Next stop, the Razum Quarry

RAZUM QUARRY

At the beginning of this dungeon, Kisara finally joins the group. Kisara's main feature is that instead of dodging, she protects herself with a shield. When facing charging enemies, a perfect parry or her bonus attack, with the right timing, will knock the enemy down. As you progress through the dungeon, two golems will block your path to serve as a tutorial.

To continue, purify the poisonous gas using 13 SP with Kisara, then climb the stairs. On the left, you will need 27 SP to purify the gas and find 1 Opal. South of the next ladder you will find a purple chest with 2400 Gald. Go up this ladder to get 1 Resurrection Vial. Then continue to a new gas to purify for 27 SP and get 1 Powerful Cure, then advance to the very northern part of the area. Heal yourself at the circle of light, save, and advance to the next room.

BOSS: LORD DORAHIM IL QARAS

Boss Lord Dorahim il Qaras\ Level 24 \Recommended level 22-23

For this fight, it is probably best to play with a physically oriented character (Alphen, Kisara or Law). The goal is to keep the hostility up while your mages (Rinwell and/or Shionne) bombard Dohalim with spells.

Dorahim starts the fight directly by preparing his Mystic Arte. While he charges, have fun and take it out on him because he won't fight back. When he finally uses his attack, retreat and dodge the stones falling from the sky.

When Dohalim is done throwing rocks at you, he will start his infinite combos. It's best not to try to attack him during this phase as you'll probably take too many attacks and die (especially when playing with Law). Just do perfect dodges to get a few attacks now and then, and run away so he can chase you. This will allow your mages to do damage in peace while you keep him busy.

If you control Kisara, you can also try to make perfect guards to stop his combo. After a while, Dorahim will be out of breath and will give you a lot of time to attack him. Take advantage of the fact that he is totally harmless to use Alphen's strong point and do massive damage.

During the second phase of the fight, Dorahim will start casting spells, including Execution. Always make sure you have either Alphen's or Rinwell's Bonus Strike available to prevent him from using his spells.

During the fight, there is also a chance that you will get a special bonus hit when Dorahim charges (which you can also block with Kisara's classic bonus hit).

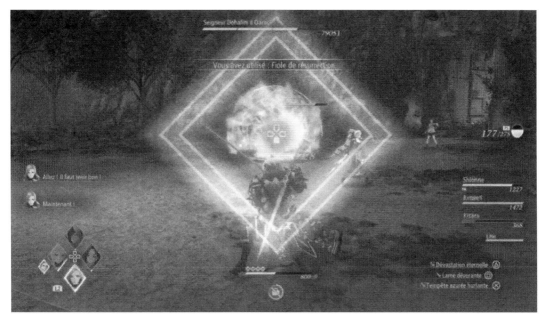

After the fight, return to the Autelina Palace to stop Kelzanik

AUTELINA PALACE

Go up the stairs to the second level. At the moment, the lord's room is inaccessible so go to the office. You will have to defeat a group of enemies with a soldier in golden armour to get there. After defeating a group of soldiers again, you will get the Key to the Noble Hall on the desk. Go to this room: after the fight you realize that there is nothing here.

So go to the barracks and/or the meeting room to see if you will have more chances there. Before you go, don't forget to take the Saffron from the room. In the barracks you will find a message on the cupboard saying that the key to the mechanism is stored "in the appropriate cabinet". In the meeting room this time you will find another message saying that the key is in the office. Go back to the office and examine the cabinet on the far southeast side.

Before continuing, go through the guard room to find 1 Topaz Plastron and the recipe for Pork Buns. In the Staff Quarters, you will find the Key to Treasures: Earth. In this treasure room, after defeating the large group of enemies, you will get 1 Elixir and 1 Evening Gown. Finally, go to the Lords' Quarters where you will find a circle of light to heal yourself, as well as the mechanism to deactivate the barrier, and face the Poisonous Lizard

Boss: Poisonous Lizard

Boss Poisonous Lizard \Level 24\Recommended Level 22 – 23

The main gimmick of the poisonous lizard is that it can teleport and become "invisible". In reality, it remains completely visible and when it becomes transparent, it makes no difference whatsoever because as soon as you touch it, it becomes normal again. His other gimmick, poison, is also something you should be well prepared for as many bosses and mobs would normally force you to create poison immune accessories.

On the other hand, he can be very dangerous if you stand in front of him as most of his attacks come either from his mouth or from a front charge. In fact, there is no point in standing in front of him as his core is on his tail so try to stay behind him at all times.

At the beginning of the second part of the fight, he will start by summoning bees as reinforcements: eliminate them as quickly as possible to avoid being overwhelmed. Throughout the second half of the fight, try to keep Rinwell's and Kisara's Bonus Strikes available to counter and knock him down when he prepares to cast a spell or make a charged attack. If Kisara's and Rinwell's strikes are not available, remember that Alphen's also works to interrupt enemy attacks.

Kingdom of Mahag Saar
TALKA POND ROAD

In the very northwest of the map you will find Red Jasmine (+10 Resistance). If you go straight ahead, you will trigger a cutscene near the lake. This will unlock the ability to fish near the ponds provided. Fishing allows you to obtain fish for cooking, to be sold, or even to obtain new titles, so don't hesitate to do a little fishing from time to time. There are also two trophies directly related to catching one, and then all the fish possible. You can click here for a much more detailed guide to fishing. Once you have completed the quest, you will unlock the title 'Seasoned Fisherwoman' for Kisara. Right next to the camp and the fisherman, you will find a soldier to heal for 31 SP. This soldier will give you 1 Infantry Shield.

MOUNT DHIARA: MOUNTAIN TRAIL

In front of you, two clawed Rioters are blocking your way: this is the opportunity for Dorahim to show his strength. His bonus attack is very effective against very fast enemies: not only will they be down for a short time, but they won't be able to dodge for a while. To finish the tutorial, you only have to use his bonus attack twice. After the fight you will get your first artefact: the crocodile crusher. Finally, you now have the possibility to have 6 Artes in shortcut and Dorahim gets the title "Treasure Hunter".

Continue straight on to find a small cave with 7300 Gald. In the cave off to the east in the middle of the area you will find 1 Stone Wing Cloak. North of the ladder towards the south of the area you will find 1 Red Sage (+100 HP). Then use the vines to climb down and enter the cave. On your way you will find 1 Person to heal with Shionne who will give you 1 Storm Beak in exchange. At the bottom of the cave, you will find 1 Mage's Cloak with wings.

Then go back to the Mountain Path, and take the southwest ladder. At the very bottom of the cave, you will find 1 person to heal with Shionne for 33 SP and get 1 Swell Stone in exchange. If you take the zigzag path to the west, you will reach the ridges. However, there is nothing you can do about it at the moment so take the other ladder to progress. Be careful: save yourself as there is a fight waiting for you in the next area.

MYSTERY SWORDSMAN

Out of nowhere, a boss fight starts. Fortunately, you are not supposed to win this fight. Just survive and try to waste as few resources as possible. Don't be too aggressive or you will pay for it very quickly. Dodge his attacks and let your teammates deal with the damage until the fight ends. Then you just have to continue straight on to the new area.

NIEZ

Once in the town, cross the bridge to trigger a cutscene, then enter the house to meet Dedyme. Once the cutscene is over, there's not much to do in Niez at the moment except for a few side quests, including getting the recipe for Roast Chicken, so you can go straight to the inn if you want. The next day, go find the owl in the north-east to get 1 Red Rose Brooch, then visit the Golden Voice to trigger the 'Unlikely Duo' side quest: it's up to you whether you want to do it now or save it for later. When you are ready to continue, take the exit to the south to get to the Este Luvah forest.

AQFOTLE HILLS

Just west of the nearest exit to Niez, you will find an owl on a ruin giving you the Retro Sunglasses. North of this owl you will find 1 Red Saffron. Before continuing to the forest, take the time to explore the other two side areas. First, head to Lake Adan, which is accessible by the path closest to Niez.

ADAN LAKE

In the north of the camp, protected by a red-eyed chameleon, you will find 1 Red Lavender. In the house to the south, you will find a person to heal with Shionne for 38 SP and get 2 Sea Bream. Then cross the lake and go through the small gate.

In this area there is first a chest containing the recipe for Bouillabaisse in the house on the left as you arrive. In the chest at the end of the passage to the left of the bridge you will find the Clapper bait. Then go straight on and beat the chameleon in the centre of the tower to get the Sealing Blade. Finally, go down to the platform in front of the tower to reach the owl giving the Angry Glasses. You can now head to the other area you have to explore before entering the forest.

RUINES D'ADAN

As soon as you arrive you will find 1 Red Chamomile to the west of the entrance. Go straight ahead and then, just past the first group of enemies, look to your right to see an owl in the distance which will give you the Angel Wings. Then climb down the ladder on the other side to find the Surface Mirage bait, then jump down the well to find the recipe for Ice Cream. You have now obtained all the important collectibles in the area. You can continue on to the next area if you wish, but there's nothing you can do there at the moment so it's time to finally go into the forest.

ESTE LUVAH FOREST

When you arrive, you will notice a lift across the street but you cannot use it at the moment. Go north and then down all the ladders. First go straight ahead to find a chest containing 8500 Gald. Then head east to find the generator to activate the lift.

First, go to SS level 3. Go north to find 1 Ring of Protection, then go to the star on your map. You will find a second generator to access level SS1, your next destination.

To the very east of the SS1 level you will find the Magic Tunic. To the far north are 2 Lizard Ridges. You can now choose one of the three options to drop from the central platform. By dropping from the north-east platform you will drop to the SS2 level with the three accessible areas. Go all the way north to find Red Verbena, all the way east for 2 Hard Spherical Shells, and all the way west for the last generator to go to all levels with the lift. Return to level SS1, and fall from the southwest, heal yourself and save before continuing as a boss fight awaits.

BOSS : TEMARARUS

Boss Temararus\ Level 28 \Weakness Dohalim's bonus strike\Recommended level 27 – 28

Temararus is an opportunity for Dorahim to shine thanks to his bonus strike. Indeed, the boss is very fast and moves in all directions. Thanks to Dorahim's Bonus Strike, not only will you knock him down, but you will also prevent him from dodging your attacks for a short time.

Once slowed down, it will then be much easier for you to get behind him and focus on his core. Again, try to take a physical character (Alphen, Kisara or Law) to act as bait when Temararus is not immobilised. This will allow your mages (Shionne, Rinwell, and even Dohalim) to attack safely.

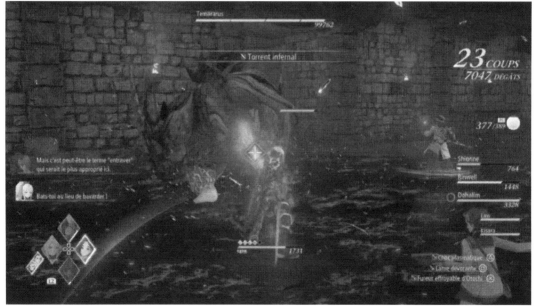

At the beginning of the second phase, Temararus will summon two Clawed Rioters: eliminate them as quickly as possible to avoid being overwhelmed. Again, Dohalim's Bonus Strike will work wonders (Alphen's works too).

Once alone, the fight is exactly the same as in the first phase. Just be careful when he goes into Out of Bounds. It is best to retreat and wait for the storm to pass during this phase, before resuming the offensive when it exits the Out of Bounds phase.

After the fight, return to Niez and rest at the inn. Make sure you're ready before you rest because another boss fight is waiting for you right after.

BOSS : GRINYMUK

Boss Grinymuk \Level 29\ Weakness Earth\ Recommended Level 27_29

Since Grinymuk is weak to Earth, this makes Dohalim, Kisara and Alphen a great asset in this fight.

Have Dohalim spam Stalagmite and/or Gravisphere, Kisara "Incandescent Emission", "Slag Attack" and/or "Crescent Moon", and Alphen "Destruction" and/or "Natural Devastation" depending on the Artes you have available. As a reminder, you can force the AI to use certain Artes by unchecking all the others. With the title "Bibliophile", Rinwell can also inflict extra damage to dragons with the skill activated.

As always with large monsters, the most effective solution is to hide behind them and attack them from behind, especially since Grinymuk has a core on his tail. He also has another one in his mouth, but it's not clear that the risks involved in reaching him are worth it. However, when you manage to knock him down (with Alphen's Bonus Strike for example), don't hesitate to go for the head rather than the tail as you will do much more damage by hitting the head.

Although it is much easier to approach him from behind than from the front, don't stick to his backside as he has many ways to defend himself. He can actually turn around with a tail strike, or plant his tail in the ground and create a tornado. The best way is to place a combo of three - four Artes, then back off when he is about to defend himself. Meanwhile, your mages, especially Dohalim, can attack him safely.

During the second phase of the fight, Grinymuk can go off-limits, during which time he can jump a long way to fall right in front of you and let out a roar that deals heavy damage. As with all boss off-limits, keep your distance and wait for the storm to pass. For the rest of the fight, keep the same technique: stay behind to avoid his bites and lasers, but don't stick him too far back either, and above all, trust your mages to do damage over time while you dodge hits and divert attention.

After the fight, Law gets the title "Mediator". Then return to the Ruins of Adan and enter the Secret Port to take the lift. Once on the pier, you will find 1 Powerful Cure in the east in a chest. Then go and talk to the person on the western quay in front of the ship and board. While waiting to catch up with the lord's ship, talk to all your teammates to see how they are doing, then talk to Mahavar again.

MOBILE FORTRESS GRADIA

First of all, you should know that everything in this dungeon is not missable. This is important to mention because the dungeon will disappear once the boss is defeated. In fact, all the loots, chests and the owl present will be moved elsewhere on the map, but are in no way lost.

Immediately on the right are 3 Resurrection Vials. Take the first one on the left, then use 19 SP to get through. Then enter the first room to the north to find 10200 Gald. Then enter the second room to the south. Defeat the red soldier, get the Access Key A and return to the elevator to use it.

You then have access to several new floors which we will explore in order. On the lower level, you will find 1 Happy Vial to the northwest of the left room and Access Key B to the southwest of the same room. In the right room, sacrifice 39 SP, defeat the chameleon and the yellow soldier, and collect 1 Magic Emblem and 1 White Cloak.

On level C2, head west first to collect the owl which can be missed. On the way, pick up the Red Saffron in the second room to the north. The owl is in the next room on a desk and gives you the Butterfly Wings. In the last room to the north, you will have to sacrifice 39 SP to get 1 Natural Cloak.

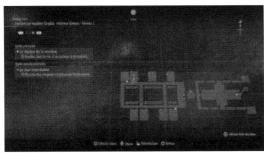 

In the rooms to the south you will find the mechanism to deactivate the red barrier that you saw at the beginning. In the next room you will find 11550 Gald. Finally, in the first room to the south, you must sacrifice 39 SP to get 1 Ring of Resistance. Before you go to where the star tells you to go, get the Elixir in the northeast behind a wall requiring 39 SP.

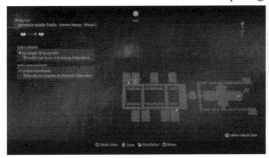 

After inspecting the lord's quarters, remember to take Access Key C from the couch, then return to the lift to climb to level 4. Here you will have to defeat the Vandal Dragon which is just in front of the mechanism to unlock access to level 3. Before you leave level 4, make sure you collect the Knight's Armour in the north-east of the area. Return to level 3, heal yourself, save, and prepare for battle against Lord Almeidrea.

Boss: Lord Almeidrea and Mesmald

Boss Lord Almeidrea and Mesmald\ Level 30 \ Recommended level 30

For this fight, unless you are very comfortable with aerial combat, you should not hesitate to rely on your mages (Shionne, Rinwell and even Dohalim) to do damage. Indeed, Mesmald is particularly mobile and its tail is difficult to reach as it moves in all directions. When he is in the air, prioritise dodging his spells rather than taking unnecessary risks to try and place three hits on his tail that will do no damage. Meanwhile, your mages will be able to do the job effectively.

Shionne will be particularly useful in this fight, as she always is when facing a flying enemy. In fact, don't hesitate to relegate the healing work to Dohalim and let her be more offensive, or even control her yourself. Rinwell, with his title 'Bibliophile', has a skill that allows him to do more damage to dragons, which will also come in handy for this fight.

If you really want to play with a physical character, wait until Mesmald is back on dry land to really attack him. In this case, instead of aiming at the tail, aim directly at the core in the mouth to do more damage. Also remember to use Alphen's Bonus Strike to knock him down.

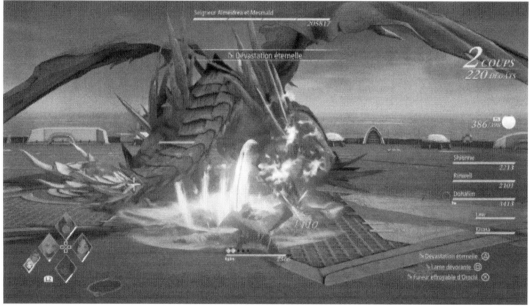

Also make sure you have Rinwell's Bonus Strike ready to use when Mesmald is about to cast a spell so you can knock him down and steal his spell.

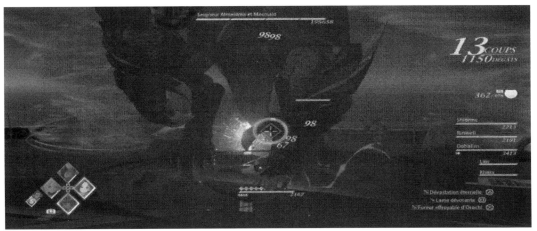

In the second phase, things will get much more complicated: Mesmald and Almeidrea will split up, which means that you now have two very aggressive bosses on the field with attacks in all directions. If there are two life bars displayed, killing only one of them will be enough to stop the fight. Obviously, it is better to choose Mesmald since he has already lost half his life. As in phase 1, always make sure you have Rinwell's Bonus Strike available to avoid being bombarded with spells by Almeidrea.

The good news is that now Mesmald spends most of his time on the ground, which makes him much easier to attack if you're playing a physical character. Make sure you keep his hostility so he doesn't attack your mages. The bad news is that Mesmald and Almeidrea can temporarily get together to prepare their Mystic Arte. When they cast it, stop attacking and just dodge the tornadoes so you don't die. Once the storm has passed, you'll only have to finish Mesmald to win the fight

Both Mesmald and Almeidrea use only air attacks. In fact, if you encounter difficulties during this fight, don't hesitate to create Opal accessories that reduce air damage by 50%.

After the fight and the long cinematic, you control Alphen in a sort of Flashback. Just go straight ahead, then talk to the people with a star above their heads, then go back to your room to return to the present, to the Kingdom of Ganath Haros.

Kingdom of Ganath Haros

TUAH COAST

When you regain consciousness, you find yourself alone in unknown territory. For now, you have no choice but to continue straight ahead. You will then have to face 2 Foam Shells alone so don't be too aggressive. Also note that you can no longer charge your attacks as you no longer have the flaming sword. After the fight, you meet up with Rinwell and Dohalim and Rinwell gets the title "Retired Avenger". Before you move on to the next area, an owl is on the right and gives you the Right Eye Hide.

THISTLYM

In the village, talk to Kisara and Law. Once the cinematic is over, leave the inn and talk to your party. Before returning to the inn, open the chest in the sea to get 1 Resurrection Vial. As you approach the inn, Zeugles will attack the village. Law also gains the title "Exceptional Fighter,

Exceptionally Left". You then head towards the capital of the kingdom. Before you continue, collect the owl on the left side of the exit and get the Star Bars

WOOD OF THE BRIGHT WATERFALL

In the centre of the area you will find a bridge that you can walk on. It allows you to reach the owl that gives you the right bandage. Behind a ruin east of the campfire in the north of the area you will find 1 Red Lavender. As you approach the wooden bridge at the very end of the area, the game will force you to rest. Then move on to the next area.

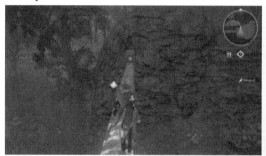 

AUREUM WATERFALLS

Progress through the waterfalls to the middle level, and head south to find 1 Golden Jelly. Then go up to the waterfall level and head south again to find 13500 Gald. Take the path south of the ladder to the top level, defeat the group of enemies and collect 1 massive breastplate. On the top level you have the option to destroy a rock for 41 SP and get 1 Earth Cloak. Continue the climb until you reach the merchant and the circle of light. Heal yourself and save because a boss fight is waiting for you.

BOSS: MERIA PHEIN

Boss Meria Phein\ Level 33\ Weakness Earth\ Recommended level 31 – 32

Meria Phein being weak to Earth makes Dohalim, Kisara and Alphen great assets for this fight. Have Dohalim spam Stalagmite and/or Gravisphere, Kisara "Incandescent Emission", "Slag Attack" and/or "Crescent Moon", and Alphen "Destruction" and/or "Natural Devastation" depending on the Artes you have at your disposal. As a reminder, you can force the AI to use certain Artes by discarding all the others.

Meria Phein is vulnerable to three types of Bonus Strikes: Shionne's when he is in the air, Kisara's when he uses his charged attack by sticking his beak into the ground, and of course Alphen's like all the enemies. This gives you many opportunities to knock him down, so try to manage your bonus strikes well so that you can use them when the time comes.

Concerning his attacks, nothing special to report: just be careful if you attack him head on to break his core not to stay stuck to him for too long or he will quickly make you regret it. Be satisfied with three or four hits / Artes and then back off. Let your mages do damage from a distance during this time (especially Dohalim with his earth spells). If you control Kisara, you can be a bit more reckless if you feel comfortable with the perfect guard. Again, your poison immune accessories will be of great help to avoid getting caught up in dodging the poison puddles on the ground.

After going off-limits, Meria Phein gains an aerial attack that you will have to avoid at all costs as it will probably be a one-shot otherwise. When he flies up and prepares to fire laser beams, look at the ground to see the laser path and get out of the way of the direction they are going to take. Some of your allies will probably stay there because the AI won't react as well as you do, but you'll just have to revive them afterwards. For the rest, the combat remains the same so you just have to keep applying the same techniques to defeat the boss.

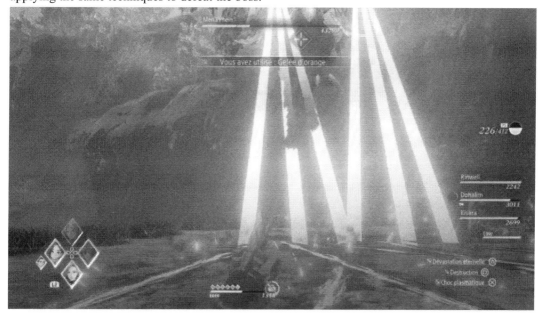

After the fight, continue your ascent. You can choose between two paths: the one on the right consists of jumping into the void and going down the entire waterfall to obtain 1 Red Rosemary. Don't worry, there is a ladder that allows you to climb back up very quickly and you will even find 1 Powerful Remedy at the top, then 1 Hell Drum a little higher up.

SWAMP OF LAVTU

When you get to the swamp, climb the vines collecting as many resources as you can to reach the upper part of the area. Head south to find the Stick Lure in a chest (you have to stand in front of it and jump to get to it). Then go up to level 3 of the swamp, and go all the way south. Before you go down the ivy, look to the right to see the owl giving you the Swirl Glasses. At the bottom you will find 1 Red Sage. All the way north in the water, behind a wall, you will find 10000 Gald. Then rest at the campfire and enter the city.

PELEGION

In Pelegion, take the lift to level 2, then level 3. Enter the palace and continue straight ahead. A fight will then start against some thorns. They are not dangerous and after killing some of them, a cutscene starts. Shionne joins the group again and you get the weapon 'Shadow Aster' and a 'Dark

Robe'. Then go to the Vholran estate.

DHEL FHARIS CASTLE

As soon as you arrive in the castle, a fight against four soldiers begins. You'll notice that now you can perform the mystical Arte "Glowing Pillar" with Alphen thanks to the new power of his flaming sword. Then go up the stairs, defeat the soldiers, and go to the next room.

Beat the soldiers on your way and continue straight on as you need to lower the bridge to go right. In the next room you will find 14100 Gald on the left. Then use 21 SP to melt the ice wall. In the northwest room is a chest containing 1 Jet Black Pourpoint. Then continue north.

In the North Tower you will find 1 Red Chamomile in the North room and 1 Elixir in the South room (you will be attacked by a large group of enemies once the chest is opened). Then continue east and climb the stairs. At level 3 you can go south and use 64 SP to get an Omega Elixir. Then continue your ascent.

On level 4, a Polycephus surrounded by two guards will block your way. Unlike the giant Zeugle version, the element of this one is wind and earth. Continue on your way to find the central entrance square (level 4). You will find the lever to lower the bridge and 3 Resurrection Vials further down the platform. Activate the lever and jump back to level 1.

You notice that the bridge is still not lowered. This is because you need to find another mechanism. Go back to the Main Tower, but this time go south. In the South Tower level 1, you will find 15500 Gald in the room to the very north. In the next two rooms you will find 1 Battle Armour, 7650 Gald and 3 Oxen. In the north you will need 64 SP to get 1 Silk Cloth.

In order to continue your ascent, you will have to beat a Polycephus again. You will then find the second mechanism that you just have to activate to lower the bridge. Right next to the mechanism is 1 Powerful Cure. Again, you can jump down to go straight back to level 1 and pass the bridge. Go up to level 4 and just behind where the circle of light is for healing, you will find the owl giving you the Hootle Doll. Heal yourself and save for the next battle.

BOSS : KALMARZEL & KALDINZEL

Boss kalmarzel \Level 34\Weakness Darkness\Recommended level : 31 - 33 depending on the chosen difficulty

Boss Kaldinzel \Level 34\Weakness Fire\Recommended level:31 - 33 depending on the chosen difficulty

For the first part of this fight, Kalmarzel is weak to darkness, which makes Shionne and Dohalim very handy for this phase of the fight. Kalmarzel is particularly sensitive to Curse status, so don't hesitate to spam "Gravity Field" with Shionne (especially since she has many titles that allow her to facilitate and increase the effects of status alterations), and "Negative Portal", "Bloody Howl", or even "Execution" with Dohalim. Since alters are cumulative, you can even try to keep the Paralysis and Poison inflicting Artes with Shionne to further annihilate Kalmarzel.

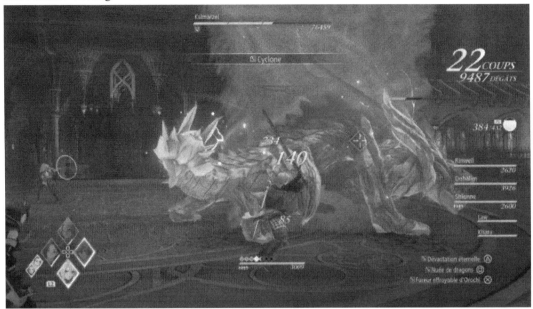

If the fight seemed too easy, don't worry, a second one arrives as soon as the first one has lost half its life. This one is weak to fire, and completely immune to dark attacks. For the time being, it's best to ignore him and finish the first Kalmarzel as quickly as possible, as with two bosses on the field, things can quickly go wrong. Use Alphen's Bonus Strike as often as possible to take him down, and Rinwell's Bonus Strike when he is preparing to cast a spell.

If you thought that once the first Kalmarzel was down, you'd be able to focus on the second, unfortunately the two merge to become even more powerful. However, Kaldinzel is still weak to fire, which is a big deal for Alphen and Shionne (and, to a lesser extent, Law and Kisara). By the way, don't forget that you can bring another character into the field at any time, so don't hesitate to bring out Dohalim for Kisara or Law for example.

Despite the transformation, the principle remains the same: use Alphen's and Rinwell's Bonus Strikes at the right moment and, when Kaldinzel is down, use Alphen's strong point to inflict massive damage.

After the fight, use the elevator while taking the Omega Elixir and the Golden Jelly on the way. Heal yourself and save again because the fight against Lord Vholran is waiting for you.

LORD VHOLRAN IGNISERI: FIRST PHASE

Boss Lord Vholran Igniseri\ Level 35\ Recommended Level 34

Similar to Dohalim during his boss fight, Vholran is very fast when he attacks and his combos seem endless, leaving you with little respite once he's done with his never-ending combo. The easiest way to do this is to play a physical character (Alphen, Law or Kisara), and act as a bait for Vholran to chase you. Meanwhile, your three mages (Rinwell, Shionne and Dohalim) bombard him with spells. This way, you will be able to lower his life bar quickly enough without taking too many risks. If you want to attack, do it only once he has finished his combo: he will then have an animation during which he puts away his sword and becomes totally vulnerable.

In addition to Alphen's Bonus Strike allowing you to take him down at any time, also keep Rinwell's Bonus Strike in reserve to counter the moment he is about to cast a spell. When he's down, use Alphen's Strength and sacrifice as many HP as possible to do massive damage.

Vholran is quite sensitive to state alterations, so don't hesitate to make Shionne a more offensive element during this fight and relegate the healing to Dohalim. If you manage to cumulate the curse, the poison and the paralysis on Vholran, the fight will become much easier at once. This requires either controlling Shionne yourself (which will be difficult, as Vholran won't let you out of the fight), or disabling all of Shionne's Artes except those that can inflict state alterations. On the other hand, freezing doesn't seem to work on him (on the contrary, he can inflict it on you).

During the second part of this first phase, Vholran can now use his Mystic Arte. When he does, don't attack him anymore and just dodge the water jets on the ground. Keep running because Vholran will not stop chasing you while he is using his Mystic Arte. You will then just have to finish him off and move on to the second phase of the fight.

As you will have noticed, most of Vholran's attacks are water attacks. So don't hesitate to create Garnet accessories that reduce water damage by 50%.

LORD VHOLRAN IGNISERI: SECOND PHASE

Boss Lord Vholran Igniseri \ Level 36\ Recommended Level 34

Basically, the fight is more or less the same, so all the tips mentioned for the first phase are still valid for the second: be the bait, let Shionne apply as many alterations as possible, and use Alphen's and Rinwell's Bonus Strikes at the right moments to be able to use Alphen's strong point and inflict massive damage.

On the other hand, during the second part of this second phase, he gains a new, much more dangerous Mystic Arte. This covers the whole area: to avoid it, you'll have to watch carefully where the stalagmites appear and avoid them by walking. Stay as far away as possible to see them coming and have time to react.

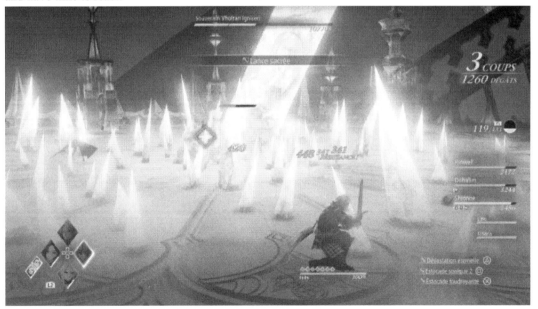

The Anchor

LIBERATION OF THE PEOPLE OF PELEGION

After the long cutscenes, Alphen unlocks the title 'The Power of the Ruler' and Kisara 'Idealist'. Return to Shionne on the rooftop observatory, then to level 3 of Pelegion (yes, you have to walk back through the castle, but jumping down from level 4 to level 1 directly doesn't take that long).

After finding your comrades, you realise that some of the people are manipulating others. Go back to the castle to try and find out more. Go back to the main tower and talk to the soldier. Defeat them and then return to the man who asked for your help. Once the dialogue is complete, Kisara will be awarded the title 'Benevolent Shield'.

Then go to level 1 of Pelegion to help another inhabitant. Go and tell the bad news to the mother on level 2, then go back to the Lavtu swamp to help her. Finally return to the inn to rest.

The next day, question the locals to find a way to reach the other kingdoms. Then return to the swamp and take the northern exit to the mountains of Forland.

THE MOUNTAINS OF FORLAND

Just before you can enter the mountains, a fight with four soldiers breaks out. Once the soldiers are defeated, enter the cellar. Continue on until you can turn into the rooms to the west: you will find the Hamburger recipe and the Sapphire Robe. In the off-centre area to the east is the Bienfu Decoy. Finally, break the rock for 43 SP and find a Bracelet of Power.

Once you are on the northern hiking trail, you will find Red Saffron on the first right, then 3 Resurrection Vials on the second left. Finally, at the bottom of the path to the far northwest, you will find 1 Sapphire Plastron. You can then return to the Frozen Valley. Activate the lever to lower the bridge and create a connection between the realms. To find the boat you need, return to the Secret Port in the kingdom of Mahag Saar. Once you reach your destination, Rinwell gets the title "A Fine Perception".

ANCRE

Inside the Anchor, start by climbing the ivy on the left to get 1 Curse Charm, then go up and take the first right to get 2 Large Semi-Human Greenhouses. Finally, take the exit to the far north to go to the lower level and use the ivy to the west to go to the upper level.

On the central level, climb the ivy just outside the door to find 1 Red Lavender, then go through the large green door. In the shaft, head west first, and sacrifice 45 SP to get 1 Ring of Endurance. Similarly, in the centre, sacrifice 45 SP to get a Ring of Resurrection. In the second room on the right is 1 Elixir and in the second room on the left is 16750 Gald. You can also activate a fast travel point before going through the door.

Continue to the middle level and, before using the ivy to climb, open the chest just beyond to get the Royal Cloak. In the shaft of spiral 4, sacrifice 46 SP twice to get 1 Bloody Cloak and 1 Spirit Bracelet. Then continue up spiral 4. On the last floor of this spiral, you will have to defeat two Armatus in order to pass. Once you reach the central core, heal yourself and save to prepare for the fight against Eljarania.

Boss: Eljarania

Boss Eljarania \Level 41\Weakness Air\Recommended level 36 - 39 depending on the difficulty

This boss is literally a copy and paste of Zacarania from chapter 3 in the Kingdom of Menancia. In fact, you can reapply exactly the same strategy, i.e. spamming wind attacks with Alphen, Rinwell, even Law and Kisara, equipping poison immune accessories, concentrating on the tentacles at first, and finally unleashing yourself on the central part of the monster. The only difficulty in combat may eventually come from the fact that, if you don't fight all the monsters on your way, nor do any side quests, you may start to find yourself a little out of level so if you feel that it's starting to get a little tight, feel free to do some side activities before continuing.

During the second phase of the fight, when the montitentacles appear, focus on them to regain control of the situation.

Once the fight is over, you just have to get out of the dungeon and go back to the port. You can use the activated teleporter on the way up to go faster. Once on land, return to Ulzebek with the fast trip and talk to Nayth, who informs you of your next destination: Berg. To get there, you will have to return to the Zionne Mine Tunnels. Take the new path available. You are now on your way to the Berg Volcano.

Daeq Faezol

BERG VOLCANO

Going to the right, you will find 1 Gothic Dress guarded by a large group of enemies. Then turn around and head left, you will unlock Dorahim's field action: sacrifice 23 SP to climb the wall. Continue, then go down and east to find a chest containing 17200 Gald. If you continue to the right, you will see a red chest guarded by many enemies containing Brigandine.

In the eastern part of the area, you can build a bridge against 47 SP to get 1 Mystic Cloak. Opposite, you can go down to collect 1 Red Sage. Then continue west to find a chest containing 1 Golden Jelly. You can then go to the lower level. Continuing straight ahead, you will have to sacrifice 47 SP to get the Absolute Armour and then 47 SP to create a shortcut leading directly to the next area. Heal yourself and save before the boss fight.

BOSS : EFRIT MALUM

Boss: Efrit Malum\ Level: 47\Recommended level :40 – 42

If you haven't had enough of hitting the flaming Zeugle, rest assured! The entire boss fight is about doing exactly that, except that a giant monster can one-shot you from the background. In concrete terms, you will have to defeat three waves of monsters in order to end the fight. The monsters are exactly the same as the ones in the zone, so pull out your best Water Artes with Alphen, Shionne and Rinwell, and do exactly what you did throughout the dungeon.

Several things though: for one thing, the monsters seem to have a lot more life than normal, or are at least a lot tougher. Above all, always keep an eye on what Efrit is doing in the background, because the slightest of his actions can eventually knock you out and if it hits the whole team, it's game over. All his attacks are very slow so they are easy to avoid, but with lots of monsters around, it's easy to forget he's there.

Once the three waves of enemies have been eliminated, you'll have to survive a few of Efrit's attacks before a special bonus strike triggers itself and ends the fight.

After the battle, you will get a Secret Key. Continue your quest for the spaceship by heading north. After finding the ship, go camping to rest right across the street. During the night, check on Shionne to see what she is doing by herself. After the cinematic, talk to all your teammates, then get into the ship. Once inside, talk to all your teammates again.

LENEGIS

After arriving on Lenegis, start by leaving the boarding area. Once in the town, talk to the locals to get more information. As you pass by, you will find a Person to heal with Shionne for 54 SP, who will in turn give you the recipe for Deluxe Parfait. Once you've spoken to all the locals you can, you can set off for the Forbidden Zone.

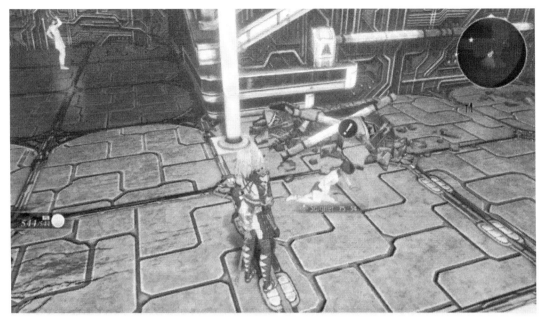

On the way, the side quest "The Renians and their Lords" will automatically start. This quest simply involves talking to 5 NPCs so take the time to do it. After completing the quest, walk through Residential Area 4 to the public garden, then continue to the next one.

From now on, you will have to fight enemies again to progress. As soon as you arrive, you will be attacked by guards. Unfortunately, the fights will be quite difficult to avoid because of the way the dungeon is built. Continue to progress until you find a chest in a small area to the east that contains the recipe for Shortcake. Continue on and eliminate the giant praying mantis as you go, then head west first to find ores and 1 Red Sage. Finally head east, collect the 21600 Gald from the chest, and move on to the next area. After the vision, heal yourself, save, and prepare for battle.

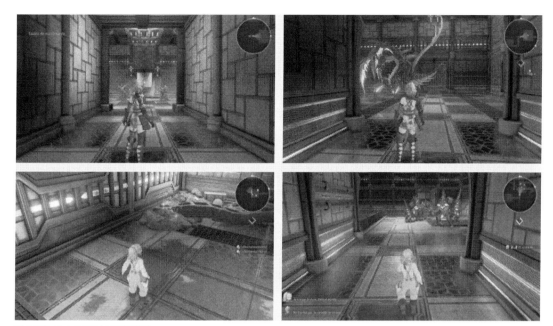

BOSS: LASER DEMON

Boss: Laser Demon\ Level: 45\ Weakness: Light\ Recommended level: 41 – 43

The boss's light weakness will come in very handy as it will allow Alphen, Rinwell and Shionne to do huge damage. The Boss is also very susceptible to stun, making Shionne a real must-have for this fight.

As far as bonus hits go, the Laser Demon has a charged attack that can be countered by Kisara. The boss phones in his attack by causing a red aura to appear around him before launching. When you see him preparing this attack, get behind him, and get ready to press the directional pad to counter with Kisara (or you can just play with Kisara and do a perfect guard).

The Demon has an attack that allows him to teleport directly at you and do a lot of damage, especially if he has entered Out of Bounds. Fortunately, it is quite easy to dodge: when he teleports, he surrounds himself with a big purple ball. When he is about to reappear, the ball will appear not far from you. This is when you have to start dodging (preferably backwards) to trigger a perfect dodge.

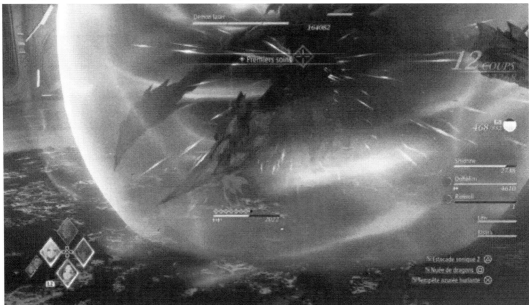

After defeating the boss, continue east to enter the Forbidden Zone.

PROHIBITED ZONE

When you arrive, Alphen will force you to visit the room on the left. Examine the control panel in the centre. Once the scenes are finished, collect the 3 Resurrection Vials and the Grape Jelly from the two side rooms, then use the teleporter to the north. In the secret area, collect the Powerful Cure in the west, then open the door. After the scene, Shionne unlocks the title "The Last Lady", and you get the Sodeil Arthalys weapon, the Gahm Arthalys armour and the Aze Phiarquis dress. Then head north to continue progressing through the Forbidden Zone. Once in the depths, heal yourself if necessary, save and prepare for the fight against the Woman in Red.

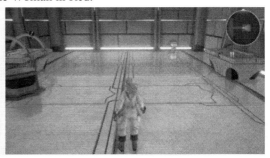

Boss : *Woman in red*

Boss: Woman in Red (x3)\ Level: 48\Recommended Level: 48 – 45

Having to deal with three enemies at the same time can make combat quite complicated. Also, they tend to attack from different directions, so if you go into hand-to-hand combat, you have a good chance of getting hit by their circular saw. Fortunately, they are quite slow (when not teleporting) so if you are not too aggressive, you should be able to land a few hits before backing off. Try to include at least two mages in the team and use the strategy option to order them to stay away from the enemies. This way, the enemies (or at least some of them) will target you, and leave the possibility for your mages to attack

A great time to do a lot of damage to them is when the three women line up to prepare a laser each. First of all, of course, don't stand in front of them or you probably won't survive. More importantly, since they are lined up, this is the perfect time to use Alphen's Bonus Strike to take down all three of them. Here, use his strong point and sacrifice as much HP as possible to damage all three at once and destroy their life bars.

When they enter Out of Bounds, once again the best strategy is to wait for the storm to pass: they will form a triangular formation and fire intersecting lasers that cover most of the arena (especially the center). The best thing to do is to stay at the ends and dodge, hoping to get a perfect dodge to do some damage while waiting.

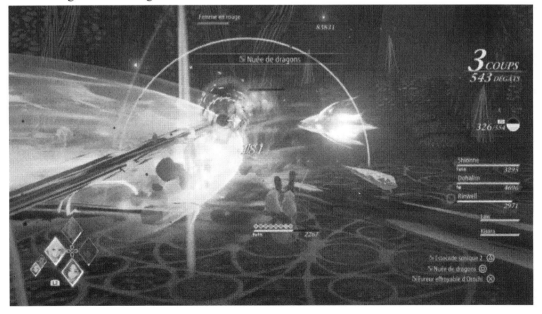

Unfortunately, you can't kill one before the others to make the fight easier since all three share the same life bar. Also, the bonus hits of the other team members won't do you much good in this fight except to extend your combos and fill your JA gauge.

Once the fight is over, leave the dungeon. After the scene, Dohalim gets the title "Chief of the Renians". Then go back to the boarding area. You will be teleported to a brand new area: take the lift in front of you and go to the central level, then go straight ahead.

When the discussion is over, go back to the lift, go to the lower level, and talk to the various people there. Then talk to the members of your group. Then return to the central level and rest so that your ship can be repaired and you can leave for Rena. Before you take off, remember to heal the person on the lower level to get 5 Happy Vials

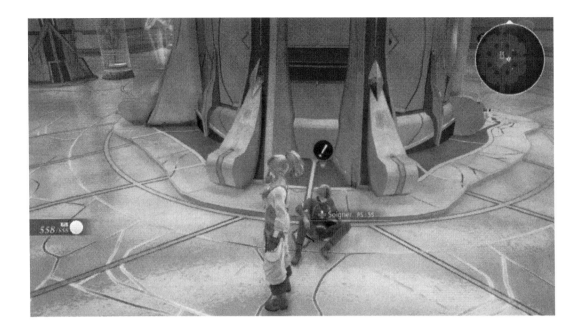

Rena

GEGHAM HELGARAHI

When you get to Rena, the only working teleporter at the moment is the one to the west, the others are shortcuts, so take that one for now. A fight against many Helganquils. Don't worry, they are much less powerful than the fight against the three women in red. Then continue south and move on to the next area

Once in the lift, use the control panel to get to level 2. You will be attacked by many enemies as you use it: be prepared as you will have to deal with several waves in a row. Then exit the lift.

In the corridor on level 2, head north and enter the room before going down: you will find a chest guarded by a Polycontrus with several wolves. The chest contains 1 Canine Pourpoint. Then go back to the corridor and go down. Pick up the Pineapple Jelly at the end and enter the room.

 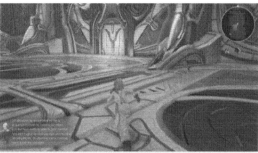

In Zone 2 of Level 2, three Helganquils will appear in your path. After defeating them, go west and use 57 SP to get 1 Sacred Cloak. Then head east and defeat the chameleon in the middle of the path to get through. On the other side of corridor 2, pick up the Powerful Cure at the end and move to the next area. Helganquils will block your way. You can then take the teleporter to the next level.

In level 1 of the Upper Level, take the first left and use 57 SP to get 1 Lucky Bracelet. Then defeat the praying mantis and Helganquils on your way to progress. Remember to get the Red Chamomile and the 2 Dragon's Bloods from the chest as you go. You can also use 57 SP to collect the Rare Plates, as well as an Elemental Cloak protected by a praying mantis and bees near the end of the area. Finally defeat the chameleon on the road, heal yourself, save, and prepare for battle.

BOSS : VALCLYNIMUS

Boss: Valclynimus\ Level :55\Weakness Lights\ Recommended level : 45 - 50 depending on the chosen difficulty

Like almost all the enemies in the dungeon, Valclynimus is weak to light. In fact, Rinwell, Shionne and even Alphen will be very useful in this fight. For most of the fight, the boss will just stay in the middle and let you hit him, defending himself from time to time without doing anything dangerous. However, sometimes he will jump up and down violently, letting out waves of darkness on the ground. When he jumps, start hammering the dodge button: if you've learned the skills that facilitate perfect dodges, chances are you'll get one without a problem, allowing you not only to dodge the attack, but also to do some damage.

The easiest way to defeat this boss is simply to use Alphen's Bonus Strike to take the boss down. When he does, sacrifice your entire life bar and decimate his. He stays down so long that Shionne will have all the time in the world to heal you. Repeating this strategy is probably the easiest and most effective way to bring him back to earth, which is important because otherwise you'll have trouble doing significant damage.

When he goes out of bounds, get out from under him at all costs as he will use his paws to crush you. Stand back and watch him do this: he will not be able to touch you until you are within reach of his paws.

After the fight, collect the Pineapple Jelly on the right just before the exit, enter the room and take the teleporter. Activate the teleporter on your way, return to refuel if necessary, then continue your exploration.

TARFHAL HELGARAHI

Right from the start, a level 55 Astral Doubt stands in your way. It is weak to light (like most of the enemies in the area) so don't hesitate to let only these Artes activate to get rid of it quickly.

At the intersection in the centre of the area, go south, use 59 SP and get 1 Fairy Ring. At the next intersection, head west first to collect 1 Mystic Emblem guarded by a group of monsters. You can then move on to the next area. Again when you use the lift, you will face many enemies so be prepared before you go up.

When you reach the lower level of Level 2 (corridor), go left to get 1 Elixir. Then take the first door on the right, use 59 SP to get 1 Ring of Endurance. Go out, climb the wall and go to the next area. Go straight ahead first, use 59 SP to find a room full of ore sources. Before returning to the corridor, defeat the group of enemies in front of the chest to get 2 Adamantine Tendons

After the cinematic, continue to area 3. Go across the street and use 59 SP to collect 1 Omega Elixir, then take the other road, defeat the dragon blocking the path and use the teleporter. Continue your climb, remembering to pick up the Red Verbena as you pass through Level 3 of Area 2.

You will eventually find the Astral Energy Convergence Zone room, a room with many generators. You will also notice a purple portal blocking your way. To get through, you only need to finish one room. With the 6 teleporters, and by defeating the enemies in the room each time, you will get 1 Will Suit, 1 Mumbane, 1 Dueline, 1 Fortress Armour, 1 Prismatic Jacket and finally 1 Wedding Dress (this last one is protected by the giant Zeugle Dancer Macabre)

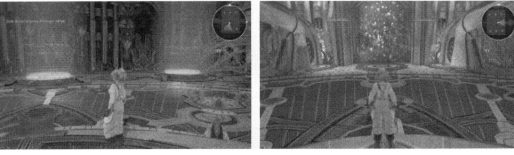

Right after that, you have the possibility to activate a last teleporter to create a shortcut, so don't hesitate to go and replenish your resources before you tackle the rooms. Be absolutely sure you're ready before you continue, because you've reached the point of no return, and there are no less than three final battles waiting for you after using the teleporter.

Boss : Great astral spirit

Boss: Great Astral Spirit \Level: 58\ Weakness: Light\ Recommended level : 50 - 55 depending on the difficulty

For the first of the three final fights, we start slowly. During this fight, the Great Astral Spirit is quite passive. Most importantly, it is weak to light. This means that you can put Rinwell and Shionne on the field, pick off any Artes that aren't of that element, and watch them completely destroy the first form of the final boss

If you want to help them with a physical fighter, take Alphen and make sure you stay away from him while a wave of darkness surrounds the Great Spirit. You will take a lot of damage and be stunned for a while.

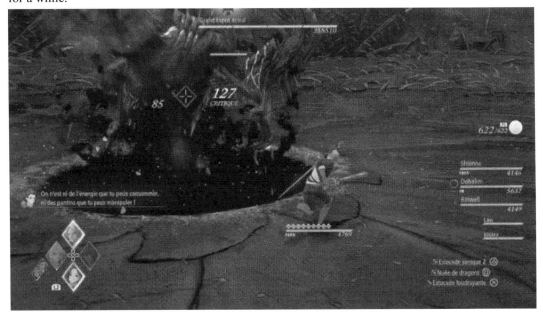

Once you've managed to get close to it, use Alphen's Bonus Strike to take it down and sacrifice all your HP to do some pretty indecent damage on a final boss.

The Great Spirit can enter Out of Bounds at any time from the start of the fight. When it does, it will teleport and throw a large ball of darkness. As long as you stay behind him, you risk absolutely nothing. Rinwell and Shionne will probably get hit as they won't be very mobile during the fight, but you'll have plenty of time to heal them (be careful not to waste too many resources though as this is only the first of three boss fights).

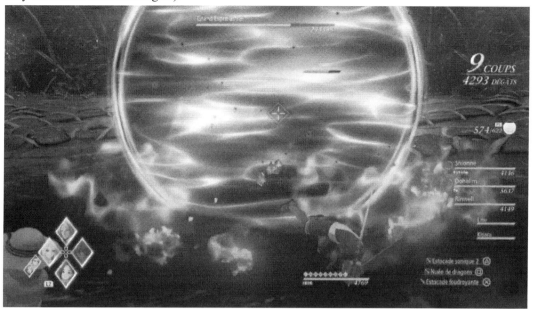

After losing half his life, four elemental balls will appear. While you can attack them and try to get rid of them, it is probably much quicker to simply ignore them and finish off the Great Spirit. Keep applying the same techniques and the Great Spirit will soon give in.

Once defeated, the latter will summon waves of Zeugle: nothing new compared to the final dungeon. So try to defeat them with as few resources as possible as you still have two battles left after that. Next step: The encompassing.

Boss : The encompassing

Boss: The encompassing/ Level 61/ Weakness: Light\ Recommended level: 50 - 55 depending on the chosen difficulty

For this second fight, the Great Spirit is already much more threatening. However, the good news is that he remains weak in the light. In fact, this means that it is still possible to use the same strategy as in the previous fight with Shionne and Rinwell, i.e. unleash all their Artes except the light ones so that they exploit the weakness permanently. Rinwell's Divine Ray will be particularly destructive in this fight

As far as hand-to-hand combat is concerned, you will only be able to hurt the boss on his arms at

first: concentrate on one at a time in order to eliminate them as quickly as possible. Be very careful: The encompassing one defends itself much more. Already, it can make columns of darkness appear where you are, so as soon as you see a circle appear under your feet, stop attacking and run away.

Most importantly, the Encompassing One can use his Black Hole Mystic Arte from the start of the fight, and this attack is not to be taken lightly. As soon as he launches this attack, just run away and dodge continuously until the attack stops. It covers more or less the whole ground so it will be very hard not to get hit, but if you have learned the skills to facilitate perfect dodges, you should be able to dodge a good portion of the attacks and survive the attack.

As far as the offensive is concerned, you can only count on Alphen's Bonus Strike to take him down, so as soon as you have the chance, use it on the arms, sacrifice all your HP, and unleash it.

Once his life bar has been halved, the weak point of The Encompassing is now on his stomach. This location paradoxically makes him easier to hit as he remains more or less motionless, unlike his arms which used to move in all directions. The second part of the fight remains more or less the same, despite the fact that he gains the ability to fire a laser straight ahead. Make sure you don't stand in front of him if he starts to roar, as the whole area in front of him will inflict darkness damage. For the rest, keep using your bonus strikes with Alphen in a relevant way and you will eventually defeat the boss.

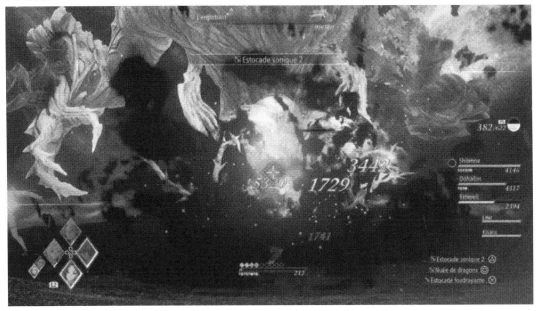

Take heart, you only have the final boss to beat!

Boss: Vholran Igniseri

Boss: Vholran Igniseri \Level 61\ Recommended level: 50 - 55 depending on the chosen difficulty

The fact that you have no teammates for the final battle (and therefore no healer) can be very scary at first. However, on the one hand, you still have the ability to use items (at least at the beginning) so if you have been careful in your use of resources, you can now let loose as this is the last fight.

On the other hand, as long as you don't try to fight (yes, it's always tempting in a Tales of), the combat is not nearly as complicated as it seems. At first, you'll notice that after each spell is cast, Vholran stays still for several seconds. This is enough time to place a few hits and 1 - 2 Artes. After that, step back and put as much distance as possible between you and him to see his attacks coming and dodge them more easily. Repeat this operation between each of his combos, no matter what spell he uses.

Secondly, and more importantly, your Bonus Hit gauge fills up much faster than normal, even without doing anything. In fact, if you're really scared of going into contact, you can just run and wait for the gauge to fill up, then use the Bonus Hit to knock Vholran down and chain him up quietly.

When he goes into Out of Bounds, avoid going into contact with him as much as possible as you will not be able to interrupt his attacks. Run away and wait for his Out of Bounds to end.

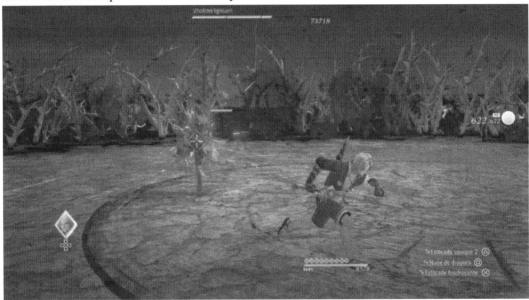

Once you have succeeded in taking half of his life, congratulations! You have already won the fight. Indeed, even if the fight resumes after the cinematic, you can't die. If you lose all your life, Alphen will enter Out of Bounds, and a special bonus hit will end the fight.

Side quests

Calaglia's side quests

In Tales of Arise, doing the side quests brings you many bonuses: money, PC, equipment, accessories, recipes, new titles for your characters... There are 70 side quests in all and, once you have completed them all, you will get the "Hero of the People" trophy. So here's how to trigger and complete all the side quests in the Kingdom of Calaglia.

THE ART OF FORGING

This quest is part of the main story and simply consists of going to the blacksmith to find out how to make weapons.

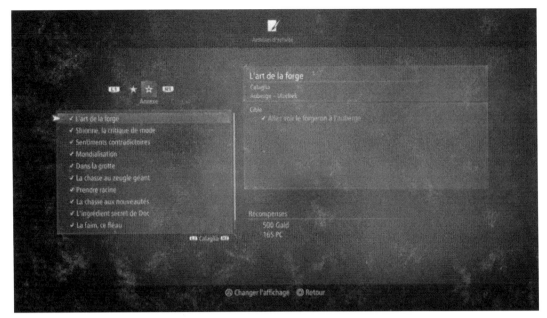

SHIONNE, THE FASHION CRITIC

Talk to the NPC in the centre of the town: whatever answer you give him, the reward and the result will be the same. It will take him a little while to find the clothes: move on in the story and, once the fifth lord is defeated, he should have them, allowing you to finish the quest.

MIXED FEELINGS

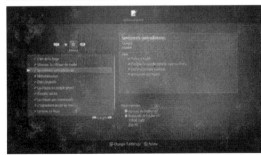 

The quest is only available after you have completed the side quest "Take Root", given by the same person. You will have to defeat the thundering Giant Zeugle.

GLOBALISATION

The quest is only available after completing the side quest "The Gourmet's Sage: Silky and Fluffy" (Ganath Haros - Pelegion - Level 2). You can buy the wheat and eggs you need at the inn in Pelegion (Ganath Haros - Level 1).

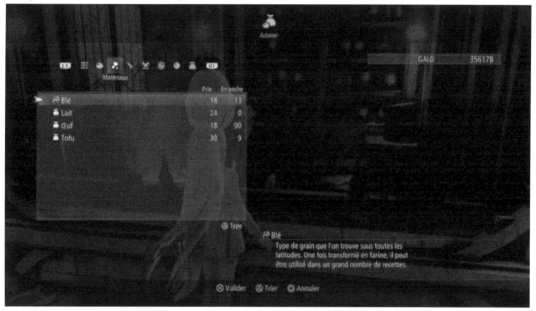

IN THE CRAFT

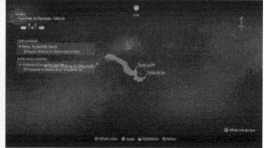

To complete this quest you must first defeat the boss Efrit Malum in the main story. Once this is done, you will get a key that allows you to open the door and get all the treasures inside.

THE HUNT FOR THE GIANT ZEUGLE

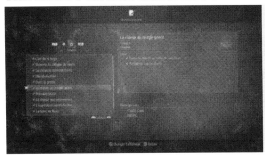 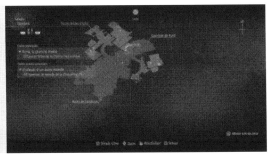

To complete this quest you will need to defeat the Giant Mantis Zeugle. As the Zeugle is level 43, it is probably wise to wait a little while before attempting to complete this quest.

TAKING RACINE

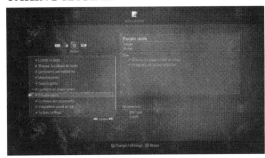 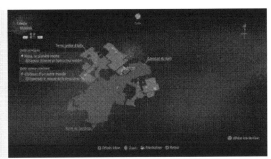

Simply defeat the wolves in the Barren Lands of Iglia to complete the quest.

HUNTING FOR NOVELTIES

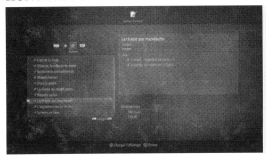 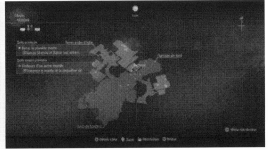

The stone fragments are a drop from the Golems found in the Arid Lands of Iglia and the Sandinus Ravine. To repopulate enemies quickly, you can simply use Quick Travel to respawn all enemies in an area and farm quickly.

THE SECRET INGREDIENT OF DOC

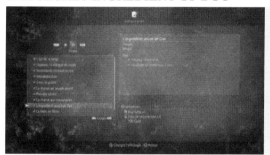

You can find all the chilli you need at the Kyrd Garrison at the harvesting points below.

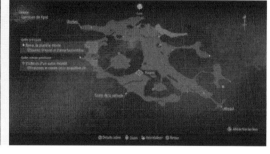

HUNGER, THAT SCOURGE

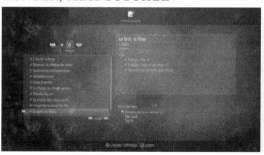
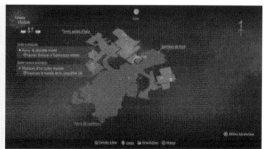

You can find the wheat and potatoes you need at the harvesting points listed below in the Arid Lands of Iglia.

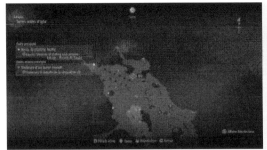 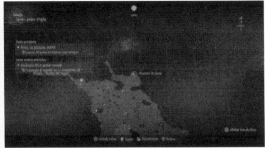

SUPPLY

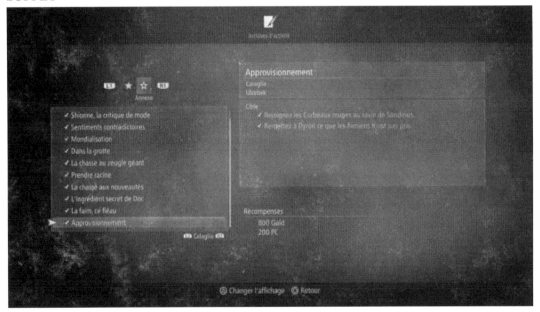

Although this is considered a side quest, you must complete it to progress in the main story. After defeating the monsters, return to Dyron to complete the quest.

Cyslodia side quests

HUMILITY LESSON

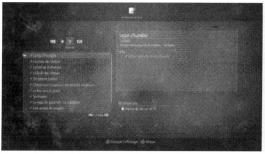
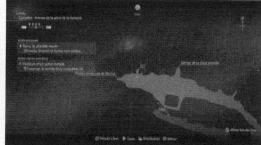

The quest is only available after completing the side quest "A Perfect World". Simply watch the scene to complete it.

THE ROAD TO THE FUTURE

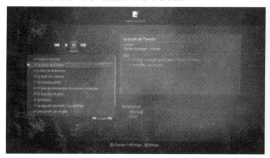
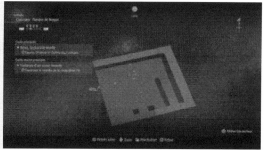

The quest is only available after completing the side quest "Grievance Book", also given by Bregon. You will have to defeat the Giant Zeugle Tumbling Montitentacle in Ulvhan's Cave.

GRIEVANCE BOOK

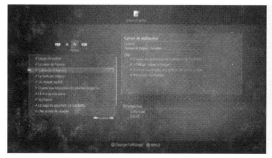
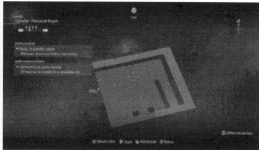

The quest is only available after you have completed the side-quest "Hunting the Snowy Plains Herds", also given by Bregon. After talking to the three people, Bregon will give you the key to open the cell in Riville's Prison Tower so you can confront the Giant Zeugle Polycephus. The cell is located in the 'Underground Prison' area.

THE OWL FOREST

 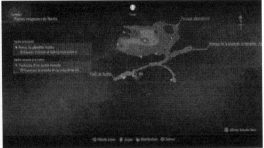

The quest starts automatically when you arrive in the Snowy Plains of Nevira, once you have discovered the owl forest. It's a long quest where you have to find the 38 owls scattered throughout the game's realms. Each owl gives you an accessory as a reward for finding it, and the owl king also gives you rewards for finding a certain number of owls. You can find the detailed location of all the owls here.

A PERFECT WORLD

 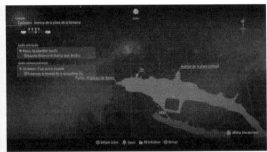

This quest is only available after defeating the four optional elemental bosses, i.e. by completing the following four side quests:

-Spiritual Temple (Menancia - Traslida Road)

-Nevira's Spectral Flower (Menancia - Library - Autelina Palace)

-Farewell, dear mage (Mahag Saar - Niez)

-A mad rage (Ganath Haros - Thistlym)

You will then only have to watch the scene to complete the quest.

SNOWY PLAINS HERD HUNTING

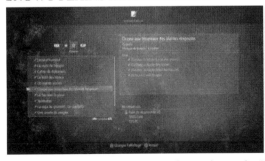 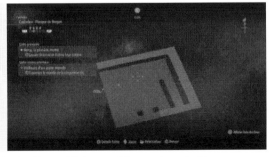

Simply defeat the three groups of enemies at the Nevira Snow Plains and then return to Bregon.

FIRE UNDER THE ICE

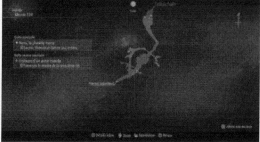

Simply defeat 7 wolves in the Silver Plains and then return to the man to complete the quest.

SPIRITS

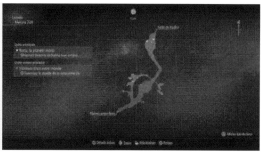

The land seeds you need are dropped by the Woodland Montitentacles you find in Ulvhan's Cave. Don't forget that to make the enemies reappear, you can simply use the Quick Trip to farm quickly.

THE GOURMET SAGA: PICKING

You can find the wheat and apples you need at the harvesting points listed below

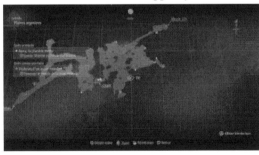
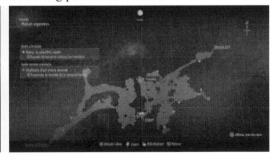

AN ARMY OF ZEUGLES

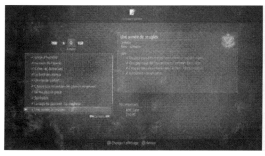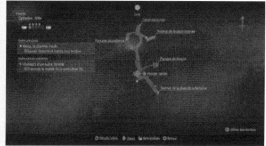

Simply defeat the three groups of enemies in the Snowy Plains of Nevira and return to him to complete the quest.

LIKE TWO DROPS OF WATER

To complete this quest, you will have to defeat the Giant Tormentor Zeugle in the Frozen Valley.

EASING TENSIONS

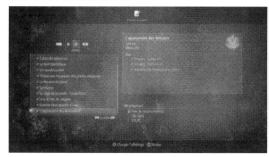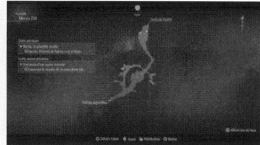

You can find your apples and lettuce at the harvest points listed below in the Silver Plains.

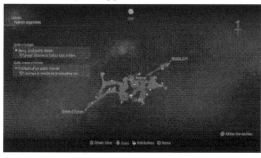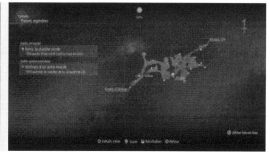

Menancia side quests

VISITORS FROM ANOTHER WORLD

This quest is only available after completing the side quest "a strange atmosphere" (Menancia -

Viscint). This quest is the traditional quest that allows other characters from past games in the series to come and play against the current cast. You will have to fight a series of bosses (six in total) from the old Tales of in order to complete this quest. You can find our detailed guide to each of the bosses you need to defeat to complete the quest here.

For each boss you defeat, you will get a character's Infernal Weapon. These are weapons whose damage depends directly on the number of enemies the character has killed.

COLLECTION OF VOICES

This quest is only available after you have started the other 69 side quests ("Visitors from Another World" and "The Memory Machine" do not need to be completed to do the quest). You will only have to find and record the voices of the different NPCs marked on your map to complete the quest).

RUST, WHEN YOU'RE WAITING FOR US

Simply defeat 8 Earth Mace (the flying enemies on the Traslida Road) to complete the quest. You can use the Quick Trip to make the enemies reappear and farm quickly.

DAHNA'S BEST PANCAKES

This quest is only available after completing the side quest "Kisara's Initiation" (Mahag Saar - Niez - Inn). Talk to the woman in the Viscint Inn, then to the farmer in the Ranch, and you will learn three different pancake recipes and complete the quest

A STRANGE ATMOSPHERE

This quest is only available after completing the main story and the side quest "Spiritual Temple" (Menancia - Traslida Road). Simply return to the Temple of the Earth Spirit to complete the quest.

FOOLPROOF DEFENCES

The granite fangs you are being asked for are dropped by wild boars on the Traslida Road and the Tietal Plain.

BOUNTY HUNTING

To complete this quest you will need to defeat the Giant Zeugle Great Dragon. The Giant is not visible on the world map: you will have to start the fight against the group of boars at the location of the green star and the Great Dragon will appear once the fight has started.

THE GOURMET SAGA: A TREAT STRAIGHT FROM THE PALATE

La quête n'est disponible qu'après avoir terminé la quête annexe "La saga du gourmet : la cueillette" (Cyslodia - Messia 224). Le boeuf, les tomates et les pommes de terre peuvent être trouvés aux points de récolte indiqués ci-dessous sur la Route de Traslida.

For mushrooms, you will find them in Viscint, near the Entrance - Gilanne Wood.

SPIRITUAL TEMPLE

This quest is only available after defeating the fifth lord in the main story. It is recommended that you wait until you are at least level 60 to do the quest as it will be very difficult if you try to do it directly. Explore the temple that appeared on the Plains of Tietal to be transported to an area where you will have to chain rooms with fights.

When you have finished all the rooms, the fight against the giant Gnome begins. It's quite similar to Efrit Malum in that you have to beat one of the waves of enemies with the real boss attacking you from the background.

THERAPEUTIC FIGHT

You only have to beat the groups of zeugles to complete the quest

THE SPECTRAL FLOWER OF NEVIRA

This quest is only available after defeating the fifth lord in the main story. In the library of Autelina Palace, approach the shelf to trigger a scene, which will launch the scene

Then go to the Snow Plains of Nevira, on the island in the centre of the lake, to start the fight against Meneiys.

DOHALIM, THE BIG GAME HUNTER

This quest is only available when Dohalim joins the team. To complete this quest you will have to defeat the Giant Reaper Zeugle alpha (Menancia - Traslida Road).

WALKING ROCK

To complete this quest, you will need to defeat the Giant Flaming Destroyer Zeugle. (Menancia - Razum Quarry - Mining Site 1).

THE BIBLIOPHILE

This quest is only available after Dohalim has joined the team. The books she asks you to show her are Rinwell weapons that you must make. Here is the list of books you have to make:

-Secrets of the Stars (Rinwell's starting book)

-The Beauty of Nature

-Taming of the Water

-Bright Light

-Divine Gaze

The ability to craft Divine Gaze unlocks very late in the adventure, so you won't be able to finish the quest until then. You will also notice that there are several versions of the books (Beauty of Nature 3 for example): just do the basic version which consumes less materials.

A HEALER AND HER PATIENTS

This quest is automatically triggered by crossing Observation Hill. Simply heal the three people to complete it.

FIELD FOR ALL, ALL TO THE FIELD

Simply go to the Training Ground east of Viscint to complete the quest

A MONSTROUS BOAR

To complete this quest, you will have to defeat the Giant Zeugle Fierce Hunter (Menancia - Traslida Road).

INVITATION TO FISH

This quest starts automatically when you cross the Talka Pond Road. Catch your first fish to complete the quest.

ONCE A RIVAL, ALWAYS A RIVAL

You will have to defeat the knight in a one-on-one duel with Kisara. The knight is level 44, so perhaps it is best if you are at his level, or even higher if you are not comfortable with Kisara, to fight him.

THE PLAINS STALLION

This quest is only available after completing the side quest "The Pharia Ranch". You only need to go to the locations indicated on your map to complete the quest

THE PHARIA RANCH

Just before you enter Viscint, you will find a man on the ground. Talk to him to find out about his ranch and finish the quest

Mahag Saar side quests
ECHOS

For this quest, you will have to defeat the Giant Ruthless Zeugle (Este Luvah Forest - Fortress Ruins - 2nd SS).

THE GOURMET SAGA: SCENT OF THE MEADOWS

This quest is only available after completing the side quest "The Gourmet Saga: A treat straight from the palate" (Menancia - Viscint). You can find the lemons, apples and lettuce at Lake Adan, at the harvesting points listed below

A WAVE OF RENEWAL

You can find the Semi-Human Muscles on the Clawed Rioters in the Este Luvah Forest. Don't forget that you can make enemies reappear with the Quick Trip to farm quickly

FAREWELL, DEAR MAGE

This quest is only available after completing the side quest "Echoes" (Mahag Saar - Niez), as well as defeating the fifth lord in the main story. It is a difficult quest so wait until you are at least level 60 - 65 to do it. You will have to go to the ridges of Mount Dhiara (Menancia). There you will find a tower: climb to the very top of the tower to face the optional boss Sylphe procella.

CLOUD OF HELL

For this quest, you will have to defeat the Giant Zeugle Mother of Bugs (Mahag Saar - Aqfotle Hills)

THE OWL SANCTUARY

After talking to the woman to start the quest, return to the Owl Forest: the correct choice is the black owl in the centre, but the answer doesn't matter as you will still get the recipe for the Sandwich at the end of the quest by returning to the woman if you give the wrong answer.

THE UNLIKELY DUO

This quest is only available after completing the side quest "A Healer and Her Patients" (Menancia - Observation Centre). Talk to the Golden Voice at the entrance to Niez and he will give you a riddle to solve. The object you are looking for is the Iron Pipe, which is located in the very north of the Arid Lands of Iglia (Calaglia).

THE INITIATION OF KISARA

As for salmon and beef, you will find salmon in the water of Lake Adan and beef on the Traslida Road (or by using the ranch).

Ganath Haros side quests

UNSCRUPULOUS FISHERMEN

The Reptilian Fists are the monkey enemies you can find at the Aureum Waterfalls. Don't forget that you can use Quick Travel to make enemies reappear and farm quickly.

THEIR FUTURE

This quest is only available after completing the side quest "The Missing Fiancé" (Ganath Haros - Thistlym). Simply talk to the knight, then go to the Temple of Saxleoh to finish the quest.

TORNADOES BY THE SEA

For this quest, you will have to defeat the Giant Zeugle Storm Catalyst (Ganath Haros - Tuah Coast)

MISTRESS OF NATURE

For this quest, you will have to defeat the Giant Elemental Zeugle (Ganath Haros - Lavtu Swamp).

A CRAZY RAGE

You will have to go through an optional area and beat a hidden boss to get the recipe. Near the camp of the Shining Waterfall Woods, you will find a patch of water where you can swim and enter a new area. Do the dungeon, beat the boss and finish the quest. Be around level 57 as the boss is not particularly difficult but has two stages.

BEYOND DEATH

In order to access the Uninhabited Island, you must start the side quest "Beyond Death". To unlock it, you must have reached the final dungeon in Rena. Come back to the Tuah Shores (Ganath Haros). As soon as you enter the area, a scene will start where you find a bottle on the ground

After that, go to the secret harbour (Mahag Saar) and show it to the person driving the boat. You have now unlocked access to the Uninhabited Island. Continue towards the green star and defeat the boss to complete the quest

THE GOURMET SAGA: SILKY AND FLUFFY

This quest is only available after completing the side quest "The Gourmet Saga: Scent of the Meadows" (Mahag Saar - Aqfotle Hills)

For Laporc meat, you will have to use the Ranch: "Raise cattle", "Send to the barn", "Laporc". Come back half an hour later to get your meat

For tofu, you can buy it from the merchant at the Pelegion hostel.

CONVERSATION WITH TILSA

Just talk to Tilsa to finish the quest: your choice does not matter.

A PLACE FOR HER

For this quest, you will have to defeat the Giant Zeugle Regent Bee (Ganath Haros - Shining Waterfall Wood).

SOME CATCHING UP TO DO

You will find the Statue Fragments infused on the Fatal Effigies (gargoyle enemies) in the Forland Mountains - Northern Hiking Trail (Ganath Haros).

THE PELEGION MASCOT

The rampaging bugs can be found at the Aureum Waterfall. There is only one group of rampaging bugs in the entire dungeon, so use the quick trip to repopulate the group after defeating them.

THE MISSING FIANCÉ

To unlock access to the quest, you must heal the soldier with Shionne in Menancia - Talka's Pond Road. Then talk to the NPCs indicated on your map to finish the quest

Other side quests

THE RENIANS AND THEIR LORDS

This side quest is automatically triggered in the main adventure, when you arrive in the residential area of Lenegis. This quest simply involves talking to 5 NPCs so take the time to do it.

THE MEMORY MACHINE

By far the biggest challenge of the game, to finish this quest you will have to defeat, in a row, without any possibility to fill your PS or to buy items :

-Balseph Ganabelt

-Dohalim

-Almeidrea

-Vholran

-All four lords at the same time (There is no Dohalim)

-Zephyr

Obviously, they are now level 95+ otherwise it wouldn't be funny... A little clarification concerning the fight against the four lords, they are not on the field at the same time : you fight them two by two, that is to say that as soon as one dies, another one takes his place, so that there are always two on the field. At the end of this gauntlet from hell is Zephyr, who returns from the dead for one battle.

Given the difficulty of the quest, don't hesitate to prepare yourself as much as possible. In fact, if you just want to finish the quest without getting bored and get the trophy/achievement for completing all the quests, the quest is doable from level 75 - 80 in story mode as the bosses don't have much life

However, if you want to do it on the highest difficulty level, you can go up to level 90 - 100 without any worries. What will make the difference is your equipment, i.e. your accessories, and your weapons. What can really help is to get the infernal weapons by doing the quest "Visitors from another world". Indeed, the more enemies you have killed with a character, the more damage they will do. So don't hesitate to farm the kills with each character to make them super powerful weapons.

Spectrum of Balseph

The entire fight takes place with the monster in the background attacking you. Create four fire damage reducing props (use "Skill Transfer" to reduce fire damage as much as possible. At this point in the game, you should be able to create props that reduce fire damage by at least 80%).

For this fight, Balseph has a charge that you can block with Kisara's Bonus Strike, giving you a chance to take him down. For the rest, avoid consuming items at all costs (except for recovering SP): this is only the first fight so avoid using them now.

Spectrum of Ganabelt

Same principle as for Balselph, create four light damage reducing props (use "Skill Transfer" to reduce light damage as much as possible. At this stage of the game you should be able to create props that reduce light damage by at least 80%).

During the first part of the fight, try to make sure that at least one of your characters never goes down to 1 HP so that they can survive their Mystic Arte Indignation because depending on the difficulty, even killing two clones will still be a knockout for everyone, especially if you don't have any light damage reducing accessories. You can also bring in a character who was in reserve while charging his Mystic Arte.

Spectrum of Dohalim

The combat here remains exactly the same as in your first encounter. It's not really worth taking the trouble to create earth damage reducing accessories since Dohalim uses mostly physical attacks. Just dodge when he attacks and go on the offensive when he gets tired. Don't forget to interrupt his charge with Kisara's Bonus Strike, and his spells with Rinwell.

Spectrum of Almeidrea

Again, create four wind damage reducing props (use "Skill Transfer" to reduce wind damage as much as possible. At this stage of the game you should be able to create items that reduce wind damage by at least 80%).

Don't miss the special bonus hit with Rinwell when Almeidrea is about to cast her Mystic Arte, because if she manages to cast it, your team will have a hard time surviving.

Vholran Spectrum

You can create accessories that reduce water damage if you wish, but this is less important than for the other lords as his attacks are still mostly physical. Above all, they can easily be dodged. Use the same technique as against Dohalim and just dodge to attack only when the opportunity arises.

Balselph, Ganabelt, Almeidrea & Vholran

It is highly recommended to ignore Balselph completely and kill him last: he is clearly the least dangerous lord so it doesn't matter if he stays on the field. As long as you don't attack him, you won't trigger the QTE that puts him in phase 2, which prevents him from dying. On the other hand, kill Ganabelt first. He's unmanageable enough on his own, and you don't want to fight him in a duo with Almeidrea or Vholran.

During this fight, you can afford to use some resources as it is the second to last one (save some for the next one anyway). You can also equip the accessories you have created to resist the elemental attacks of the lord on the field (Light when it's Ganabelt, Wind when it's Almeidrea, and finally Water or Fire when there is only Vholran and Balseph left).

Zephyr

If you've made it this far, you've done the hard part, but Zephyr is no walk in the park. While doing damage directly to Zephyr will be difficult because of his speed and damage, there are plenty of opportunities to take him down with Bonus Strikes. Indeed, in addition to Alphen, Law can also take down his father with his Bonus Strike at any time. If you add Rinwell who can steal his spells (and even Kisara for the first part of the fight), that's a lot of opportunities to take him down and inflict huge damage with Alphen. If you've managed your resources well, you should be able to defeat Zephyr and end this long, infernal boss-rush.

THE SUPER ZEUGLE

This quest is only available after completing the side quest "An Ambition Realised", given by the same person. For this quest you will have to defeat the Giant Zeugle Bulldozer (Mahag Saar - Lake Adan).

THE ULTIMATE ZEUGLE

This quest is only available after completing the side quest "The Super Zeugle", given by the same person. For this quest, you will have to defeat the giant Zeugle Ezamamuk (Menancia - Mount Dhiara - Mountain Base)

FABRIC SAMPLE

For this side quest, you will have to defeat the Giant Zeugle Walking Scourge (Rena - Gegham Helgarahi - Upper Level - Level 3).

AN AMBITION REALIZED

This quest is only available after you have completed the side quest "Sample Cloth", given by the same person. You will need to defeat a slightly more powerful than normal version of a Helganquil.

Location of owls

On this page of our complete Tales of Arise solution, you will find all our guides to the location of the 38 owls in the "Owl Forest" quest, sorted by kingdom. Each owl found allows you to obtain a cosmetic accessory for your characters to wear. You'll also find out how to get the last six special owls and the requirements for making them appear.

Owls of the Kingdom of Calaglia

OWL N°1 Location :Ravine of Sandinus \ Gift : Dog's tail

> Perched on a tree, just after the bridge leading to Ulzebek.

OWL N°2 Location : Ulzebek \ Gift : Rabbit ears

> Perched on a clothesline, you must climb the ladder inside the house to reach it

OWL N°3 Location : Arid lands of Iglia\Gift : Spotted cat ears

> To the southwest of the Iglia Barren Lands, look for the scale on your map, go up, and you'll find the owl perched on a tree at the end of the area

OWL N°4 Location : Kyrd Garrison\Gift : Cat's tail

> Near the camp at the entrance to Mosgul, go to the off-center area, and look to the left at the edge of the cliff

OWL N°5 Location : Mosgul\Gift : Monocle

> South of Mosgul, behind a brick wall

OWL N°6 Location : Flame trench\ Zone : Castle doors\Gift : Dog ears

> Turn right and look into the house on your left.

OWL N°7 Location : Flame trench\Zone : Fire doors\Gift : Left bandage

> At the entrance of the area, go to the center and then to the left : the owl will be against the wall on the ground.

OWL N°8 Location : Glanymede Castle\Zone : 3rd level\Gift : Rabbit's tail

OWL N°9 Location : Cliffs of Lacerda\Gift : Rimmed glasses

> Right next to the camp of the place.

Owls of the kingdom of Cyslodia

OWL N°10 Location : Silver plains\Gift : right eye patch

> Just before entering Messia 224, on the wall next to the bridge.

OWL N°11 Location : Messia 224\Gift : Wolf ears

> In the upper part of the village, hidden in a basket behind the ox on the left

OWL N°12 Location : Snowy plains of Nevira\Gift : Wolf's tail

> In the middle of the lake, on the small island.

OWL N°13 Location : Cysloden\Zone : Alley\Gift : Sunglasses

> Perched on a rock, at the river in the Alley.

OWL N°14 Location : Prison Tower of Riville\Zone : 2nd level\Gift : Devil horns

> Perched on a bookcase in the very southeast room

OWL N°15 Location : Frozen valley\Gift : Half circles

On the tree near the bridge leading to the upper level - Safar Sea Cave

Owls of the kingdom of Menancia

OWL N°16 Location : Observation Hill\Gift : Red tropical brooch

Just to the left of the fishing point.

OWL N°17 Location : Traslida Road\Zone : Traslida Road\Gift : Demon Wings

Hidden in the wheat field near the animals

OWL N°18 Location : Plain of Tietal\Gift : Smiling glasses

OWL N°19 Location : Viscint\Zone : Viscint\Gift : Auréole

To the east of the inn, in the middle of the merchant's store

OWL N°20 Location : Palace of Autelina\Zone : Kitchens\Gift : Crown

In the palace kitchens, on the first floor.

OWL N°21 Location : Talka Pond Road\Gift : Demon's tail

To the west near the entrance to Viscint, at the top of the wall

Owls of the Mahag Saar Kingdom

OWL N°22 Location : Niez\Zone : Niez\Gift : Red rose brooch

All in the northeast, in the middle of the bazaar.

OWL N°23 Location : Hills of Aqfotle\Gift : Retro sunglasses

In the middle of the ruins, near the entrance of the Lake of Adan.

OWL N°24 Location : Lake Adan\Gift : Angry glasses

In the middle of the area, in the water, you will find an iron gate that will allow you to access the north of the area. Continue to the tower, then turn around and go down to find the owl.

OWL N°25 Location : Ruins of Adan\Gift : Angel wings

En arrivant dans la zone, continuez tout droit puis, juste après le premier groupe d'ennemi, regardez sur votre droite pour apercevoir le hibou.

OWL N°26 Location : Mobile fortress Gradia\Gift : Butterfly wings

On level C2, in the far northwest.

Be aware that if you don't find the owl before you beat the boss of the area, the area will disappear. However, the owl is not missable because if you miss it, it will be moved to Thislym (Ganath Haros), near the sea

Owls of the kingdom of Ganath Haros

OWL N°27 Location : Tuah Coast\Gift : Right eye patch

Just before entering Thistlym, on the right.

OWL N°28 Location : Thistlym\Zone : Thistlym\Gift : Star bars

Turn left just before exiting towards the Bois de la Cascade éclatante.

OWL N°29 Location : Wood of the bright waterfall\Gift : Straight bandage

On the bridge in the center of the area.

OWL N°30 Location : Lavtu Swamp\Zone : Marécage de Lavtu\Gift : Whirlwind glasses

Just before descending the ladder at the very south of the area, on the left

OWL N°31 Location : Pelegion\Zone : Level 2\Gift : Sad glasses

> All the way to the southwest of the level. However, you will have to defeat the fifth lord first before you can get the owl.

OWL N°32 Location : Castle of Del Fharis\Zone : Central Entrance Plaza - Level 4\Gift : Hootle doll

> It is on the chandelier behind you when you find the healing circle.

Location of the six special owls

HOW TO MAKE THE SPECIAL OWLS APPEAR?

The last six owls are not naturally found in their location, so you will have to make them appear. To do this, you need to meet the following conditions:

-To have finished the story the first time (to have the star on the savegame)

-To have found the first 32 owls and to have spoken to the owl king in the owl forest.

When this is the case, a scene will start, and a message will tell you that the special owls have finally appeared.

OWL N°33 Kingdom : Calaglia\ Location : Glanymede Castle\Zone : Lord's room\Gift : Lady's Shield

> On the throne of Balseph

OWL N°34 Kingdom : Calaglia\ Location : Arid lands of Iglia\Gift : Shining sphere

Not far from where you found the first owl in this area, stick to the cliff north of this position (the place where you found the owl) to bring up the opportunity to build ivy with Dohalim for 64 SP. The owl is at the top

OWL N°35 Kingdom : Cyslodia\ Location : Prison Tower of Riville\Zone : Secret room\Gift : Broken machine gun

In order to access the secret chamber, you will have to complete the side quest "Grievance Book", obtained by first completing the quests "Snowy Plains Herd Hunt" and "Road to the Future". This quest consists of killing the giant Zeugle that is locked in the cage in the underground prison. Once this is done, you will get the secret key, letting you enter the secret chamber via the office.

OWL N°36 Kingdom : Menancia\ Location : Palace of Autelina\Zone : 2nd level - Guard room\Gift : Old excavator

OWL N°37 Kingdom : Other\ Location : uninhabited island\Gift : Miner's cap

In order to access the Uninhabited Island, you must start the side quest "Beyond Death". To unlock it, you must have reached the final dungeon in Rena. Come back to the Tuah Shores (Ganath Haros). As soon as you enter the area, a scene will start where you find a bottle on the ground.

After that, go to the Secret Harbor (Mahag Saar) and show it to the one who drives the boat. You have now unlocked the access to the uninhabited island. Continue towards the green star, defeat the boss, and you can finally get the owl.

OWL N°38 Kingdom : Ganath Haros\ Location : Castle of Del Fharis\Zone : Lord's room\Gift : Trident

Location of the Giant Zeugles

Giant Zeugles of the Kingdom of Calaglia

MANTE

Giant : Mante\ Location : Ravine of Sandinus\ Level :43\ Weakness :Air\ Recommended level :40

This is the first Giant you will encounter so it is hard to miss. On the other hand, you won't be able to face him for a while so come back when you are around level 40.

ARMADILLO POISONER

Giant : Armadillo poisoner \ Location : Glanymede Castle - 4th level \ Level :13\ Recommended level :11

TUMULTUOUS MONTITACULE

Giant : Tumultuous Montitacule \ Location : Ulvhan Cave \ Level :15\ Weakness :Air\ Recommended level :13

THUNDERING GIANT

Giant : Thundering giant \ Location : Arid lands of Aglia \ Level :53\ Weakness :Fire\ Recommended level :50

To be able to access this giant, you will have to do first the quest "Take root" and then trigger a second quest "The hunt for novelties".

Giant Zeugles of the Kingdom of Cyslodia

POLYCEPHUS

Giant : Polycephus \ Location : Prison Tower of Riville - Underground Prison \ Level :21\ Recommended level :21

In order to access this Zeugle, you'll need to complete the side quest "Snow Plains Trope Hunt" and then launch the quest "Grievance Book", both of which were given to you by Bregon at Bregon's Hideout - Cysloden. Killing this Zeugle is the main objective of the second quest, and you'll get the key to open the cage to fight him by accepting the quest

TURNER

Giant : Tormentor \ Location : Frozen valley \ Level :39\ Weakness :Air\ Recommended level :38

In order to make this Zeugle appear, you have to launch the quest "Like two drops of water", located in the Avenue de la place de la fontaine - Cysloden. Talk to the boy on the spot, who will give you the location of the Zeugle.

Giant Zeugles of the Kingdom of Menancia

FAUCHEUR ALPHA

Giant : Alpha mower \ Location : Traslida Road \ Level :25\ Weakness Earth:\ Recommended level :25

To make this Zeugle appear, you will have to start the side quest "Dohalim, the Big Game Hunter" by talking to the woman near the farm on the Traslida Road. The quest becomes available only when Dohalim joins the team for good.

RELENTLESS HUNTER

Giant : Relentless hunter \ Location : Traslida Road \ Level :26\ Weakness Earth:Air\ Recommended level :25

This zeugle appears only after you start the side quest "A Monstrous Boar" by talking to the woman in the second street on the right of the Viscint entrance

FLAMBOYANT DESTROYER

Giant : Flaming Destroyer \ Location : Razum Quarry - Mine Site 1 \ Level :28\ Weakness Earth:

Water \ Recommended level :26

To make this Zeugle appear, you will have to launch the side quest "Walking Rock" given by the man near the bridge leading to the Razum Quarry, in Viscint

BIG DRAGON

Giant : Great dragon \ Location : Traslida Road \ Level :26\ Weakness Earth: Water \ Recommended level :24

In order to make this Zeugle appear, you will have to start the side quest "Bounty Hunt" given by a man near the central intersection in Viscint.

Giant Zeugles of the Mahag Saar Kingdom

IMPITOYABLE

Giant : Merciless (x2) \ Location : Este Luvah Forest - Ruins of the fortress - 2nd SS \ Level :43\ Recommended level :43

To make this Zeugle appear, you will have to start the side quest "Echoes" which is in Niez, by talking to the man near the exit to the hills of Aqfotle.

MOTHER OF ALL BUGS

Giant : MOTHER OF ALL BUGS \ Location : Hills of Aqfotle \ Level :42\ Recommended level :40

To make this Zeugle appear, you must launch the side quest "Cloud of Hell", given by the woman at the Secret Port.

Giant Zeugles of the kingdom of Ganath Haros

STORM CATALYST

Giant : Storm Catalyst \ Location : Tuah Coast \ Level :42\ Weakness Earth: Earth \ Recommended level :39

To make this Zeugle appear, you have to launch the side quest "Tornadoes by the sea", given by the man at the entrance of Thistlym

REGENT BEE

Giant : Regent bee \ Location : Wood of the bright waterfall \ Level :45 Recommended level :42

To make this Zeugle appear, you must launch the side quest "A place for her", given by the man near the campfire in the woods of the Shining Waterfall.

ELEMENTARY

Giant : Elementary \ Location : Lavtu Swamp\ Level :42\ Weakness :Air\ Recommended level :42

To make this Zeugle appear, you must launch the side quest "Mistress of Nature", given by a little boy at Level 2 of Pelegion

Location of other Giant Zeugles

AMBULANT FLAG

Giant : Walking Scourge\ Location : Rena - Gegham Helgarahi - Upper level - Level 3 \ Level :54\ Weakness : Light\ Recommended level :55

To make this Zeugle appear, you need to start the side quest "Sample of Cloth" given by the man on the lower level of Daeq Faezol. It is necessary to have completed the side quest "An Ambition Achieved Before

BULLDOZER & FEMALE BULLDOZER

Giant : Bulldozer (x2) \ Location : Lake Adan (Mahag Saar) \ Level :56\ Recommended level :55

To make this Zeugle appear, you have to launch the side quest "The Super Zeugle", given by the same person who gave "Sample of fabric" (which implies to have finished this quest before)

DANCER OF DEATH

Giant : Dancer of Death \ Location : Rena - Tarfhal Helgarahi - Water Astral Energy Separator\ Level :56\ Weakness : Light\ Recommended level :55

EZAMAMUK

Giant : Ezamamuk \ Location Menancia - Mount Dhiara - Base of the mountain:\ Level :59\ Recommended level :60

To make this Zeugle appear, it is necessary to launch the side quest "The Supreme Zeugle", given by the same person who gave the side quest "The Super Zeugle" (which implies to have finished this quest before)

Collectibles, crafts and side activities

Location of all recipes

MEATS

Roasted chicken

Recipe : Roast chicken\ Effect : Dark mark (attracts enemies)\ Ingredient : -Chicken x1

-Chilli x1\ Favorite dish of : Alphen (+15% effect)

Reward for the side quest "A Wave of Renewal" (Mahag Saar - Niez). You must find three semi-human Muscles, drop of the Clawed Rioters.

Brochette

Recipe : Brochette \ Effect : Attack + \ Ingredient :- Leftover meat x1

-Chilli x2\ Favorite dish of : Law (duration -25%, effect +)

Reward for the side quest "Doc's secret ingredient" (Calaglia - Mosgul)

Beef stew

Recipe : Beef stew \ Effect : Recovery of HP after combat 1 (10%) \ Ingredient : -Beef x1

-Potato x2-Tomato x2-Mushroom x1\ Favorite dish of : Dohalim (+30% effect)

Reward for the side quest "The Gourmet Saga: A treat straight from the palate". You can find all the ingredients for the quest on the Road to Traslidia and Viscint (near the entrance to the woods)

Sausage

Recipe : Sausage \ Effect : Attack +III (+16%) \ Ingredient :- Pork x1-Mutton x4-Chilli x2-Horse meat x1\ Favorite dish of :- Alphen (effect +15%)-Law (duration-25%, effect +)

Reward from the side quest "In the cave" (Calaglia - Flame Trench - east side). After defeating Efrit Malum in the main story, use the key to open the door on the way to the castle. You just have to enter to finish the quest and get the recipe.

Grilled Laporc

Recipe : Grilled Laporc\ Effect : Bonus PC II \ Ingredient :- Pork x1-Chilli x2\ Favorite dish of : Dohalim (effects +30%)

Reward for the side quest "The missing fiancé" (Ganath Haros - Thistlym). To unlock the quest, you must heal the soldier in Menancia - Talka's Pond Road

Pork Brioche

Recipe : Pork Brioche \ Effect : Attack +I (+8%) \ Ingredient : -Wheat x2-Pork x1\ Favorite dish of : Law (durée -25%, Effet +)

The recipe is in a blue box in the Palace of Autelina (Menancia), in the guard room

Horse Sashimi

Recipe : Horse Sashimi \ Effect : Attack +II (+12%)\ Ingredient : Horse meat x3\ Favorite dish of : -Law (duration -25%, effect +)-Dohalim (effect +30%)

The recipe is in Niez (Mahag Saar), at the Black Wings Headquarters, in a safe

FISH

Fish in sheet

Recipe : Fish in sheet \ Effect : EXP bonus (+4%)\ Ingredient : -Lettuce x2-Sea bream x1\ Favorite dish of : Kisara (duration +20%)

The recipe is obtained automatically once Kisara and Dohalim join the team

Lohikeitto

Recipe : Lohikeitto \ Effect : Abundant booty I \ Ingredient : -Potato x2-Milk x1-Salmon x1\ Favorite dish of : Kisara (duration +20%)

The recipe is a reward from the side quest "Spirits" (Cyslodia - Messia 224). Earth seeds can be obtained from the Woodland Montitentacles (Rudhir Forest)

Fish steak

Recipe : Fish steak \ Effect : EXP II bonus (+12%) \ Ingredient :- Legendary Fish x1-Chilli x2 \ Favo-rite dish of : Kisara (duration +20%)

 The recipe is a reward from the side quest "The Mascot of Pelegion". The rampaging bugs are located at the Aureum Waterfall. There is only one group of rampaging bugs in the entire dungeon, so use the quick trip to repopulate the group after you beat them.

Sushi

Recipe : Sushi \ Effect : EXP III bonus (+16%) \ Ingredient :- Rice x3-Sea bream x1-Tuna x1-Salmon x1 \ Favo-rite dish of : -Kisara (duration +20%)-Dohalim (+30%)

The recipe is a reward of the side quest "A mad rage" (Ganath Haros - Thistlym). You will have to go through an optional area and defeat a hidden boss to get the recipe. Near the camp of the Shining Waterfall Woods, you will find a corner of water where you can swim and enter a new area. Do the dungeon, beat the boss and finish the quest. Be around level 57 because the boss is not especially difficult but has two stages.

Grilled fish

Recipe : Grilled fish \ Effect : Recovery of PS after a fight (5 PS) \ Ingredient : Carp x1 \ Favo-rite dish of : Kisara (duration +20%)

The recipe is in a safe in Mosgul (Calaglia), just north of the area.

Milling fish

Recipe : Milling fish \ Effect : Defense +III (+ 20%) \ Ingredient : -Wheat x2-Lemon x2-Flatfish x1\ Favo-rite dish of : Kisara (duration +20%)

To obtain this recipe, you must first complete the side quest "Beyond Death".

In order to access the Uninhabited Island, you need to start the side quest "Beyond Death". To unlock it, you must reach the final dungeon in Rena. Come back to the Tuah Shores (Ganath Haros). As soon as you enter the area, a scene will start where you find a bottle on the ground.

After that, go to the Secret Harbor (Mahag Saar) and show it to the one who drives the boat. You have now unlocked the access to the uninhabited island. Continue towards the green star, defeat the boss, and jump on the platform right after to open the chest and get the

Bouillabaisse

Recipe : Bouillabaisse \ Effect : Recovery of PS after a fight I (10 PS) \ Ingredient :- Salmon x1-Mackerel x1-Mushroom x1-Tomato x2\ Favo-rite dish of : Dohalim (+30%)

The recipe is in a chest at the Lake of Adan (Mahag Saar). Cross the lake and go through the small gate. The chest is in the house on the left when you arrive.

VEGETABLES

Recipe : VEGETABLES \ Effect : Elemental Defense + (+5%) \ Ingredient : Mushroom x3 \ Favo-rite dish of : Alphen (Effect +15%)

The recipe is in a safe at the Kyrd Garrison (Calaglia), in the southern outlying area.

Steamed potato

Recipe : Steamed potato\ Effect : Recovery of HP after combat (5%)\ Ingredient : Potato x4 \ Favo-rite dish of : Shionne (Ingredients used x2, Effect +90%, Duration +90%)

The recipe is a reward from the side quest "Hunger, that scourge" in Ulzebek (Calaglia).

Vegetable soup

Recipe : Vegetable soup\ Effect : Rare ore bonus 1\ Ingredient : -Tomato x2-Potato x1\ Favo-rite dish of :- Alphen (Effect +15%)-Law (Duration -25%, Effect +25%)-Kisara (Duration +20%)

The recipe is obtained automatically during the main adventure, right after you learn how to make equipment.

Vegetable juice

Recipe : Vegetable juice \ Effect : Ore bonus 1 \ Ingredient :- Lettuce x1-Tomato x1-Apple x1 \ Favo-rite dish of : Kisara (duration +20%)

Vitaminized Smoothie

Recipe : Vitaminized Smoothie\ Effect : Elementary defense +II (+15%)\ Ingredient :- Lettuce x2-Apple x1-Lemon x2 \ Favo-rite dish of : Kisara (Duration +20%)

The recipe is a reward from the side quest "The Gourmet Saga: Scent of the Meadows" (Mahag Saar - Hills of Aqfotle). You can find all the ingredients at the Lake of Adan

DESSERT

Luxury parfait

Recipe : Luxury parfait \ Effect : Elemental Attack +II (+12%) \ Ingredient :- Milk x3-Egg x3-Strawberry x5-Apple x2\ Favo-rite dish of : Rinwell (Effect -20%, Duration +50%)

The recipe is obtained by healing the injured NPC in Lenegis with Shionne (Others - Lenegis - Residential Area 16)

Apple Pie

Recipe : Apple Pie\ Effect : Elemental attack + (+4%) \ Ingredient : -Wheat x2-Apple x2\ Favo-rite dish of : Rinwell (Effect -20%, Duration +50%)

The recipe is a reward from the side quest "The Gourmet Saga: Gathering" (Cyslodia - Jelly Valley). You can find all the ingredients in the Silver Plains.

Ice cream

Recipe : Ice cream \ Effect : Elemental Attack + I (+8%) \ Ingredient : -Milk x1-Egg x1 \ Favo-rite dish of : Rinwell (Effect -20%, Duration +50%)

The recipe is in a chest in the Ruins of Adan (Mahag Saar). In the north of the area, go down the ladder into the well and open the chest.

Shortcake

Recipe : Shortcake \ Effect : Elemental Attack + III (+16%)\ Ingredient : Wheat x2-Strawberry x1-Milk x1-Egg x1 \ Favo-rite dish of : Rinwell (Effect -20%, Duration +50%)

The recipe is in a blue chest in Lenegis - Maintenance Corridor (Other), west of the area.

Pancakes

Recipe : Pancakes \ Effect : Bonus ore III\ Ingredient :- Wheat x3-Milk x1-Egg x1 \ Favo-rite dish of :- Shionne (Ingredients used x2, Duration +90%, Effect +90%)-Rinwell (Effect -20%, Duration +50%)

The recipe is a reward for the side quest "The Bibliophile" (Menancia - Library - Autelina Palace), consisting of making the Rinwell weapons requested by the NPC.

Shionne Pancakes

Recipe : Shionne Pancakes \ Effect : Post-Combat Recovery III (20%)\ Ingredient :- Wheat x3-Milk x1-Egg x1-Apple x1 \ Favo-rite dish of : Shionne (Ingredients used x2, Duration +90%, Effect +90%)

The recipe is a reward for the side quest "Dahna's Best Pancakes" (Menancia - Pharia Ranch). To trigger the quest, go to the Viscint Inn, then to the ranch, and you will get the three pancake recipes. It is necessary to have completed the side quest "Kisara's Initiation" (Mahag Saar - Niez - Inn) to trigger the quest.

Dohalim Pancakes

Recipe : Dohalim Pancakes\ Effect : Rare ore bonus III\ Ingredient : -Wheat x3-Milk x1-Egg x1-Pork x1\ Favo-rite dish of : Dohalim (+30%)

The recipe is a reward for the side quest "Dahna's Best Pancakes" (Menancia - Pharia Ranch). To trigger the quest, go to the Viscint Inn, then to the ranch, and you will get the three pancake recipes. It is necessary to have completed the side quest "Kisara's Initiation" (Mahag Saar - Niez - Inn) to trigger the quest.

Pancakes de Hootle

Recipe : Pancakes de Hootle \ Effect : Abundant booty III \ Ingredient : -Wheat x3-Milk x1-Egg x1-Strawberry x1\ Favo-rite dish of : Rinwell (Effect -20%, Duration +50%)

The recipe is a reward for the side quest "Dahna's Best Pancakes" (Menancia - Pharia Ranch). To trigger the quest, go to the Viscint Inn, then to the ranch, and you will get the three pancake recipes. It is necessary to have completed the side quest "Kisara's Initiation" (Mahag Saar - Niez - Inn) to trigger the quest.

Gladys' Donuts

Recipe : Gladys' Donuts \ Effect : PC III Bonus \ Ingredient :- Wheat x2-Egg x2\ Favo-rite dish of : -Shionne (Ingredients used x2, Duration +90%, Effect +90%)-Alphen (Effect +15%)

The recipe is a reward of the side quest "Globalization" (Calaglia - Mosgul). This quest is only available after you have completed the Gourmet Saga and thus obtained the recipe "Curry Mabo". You can simply buy the ingredients at the inn in Pelegion.

OTHER

Curry

Recipe : Curry\ Effect : Defense + II (+15%)\ Ingredient : -Rice x2-Potato x2-Beef x2-Chilli x2\ Favo-rite dish of : -Alphen (Effect +15%)-Law (Duration -25%, Effect +)

The recipe is a reward of the side quest "Kisara's initiation" (Mahag Saar - Niez - Inn).

Gnocchi

Recipe : Gnocchi\ Effect : Elemental Defense +I (+10%)\ Ingredient : -Wheat x2-Egg x1-Potato x2 \ Favo-rite dish of : -Shionne (Ingredients used x2, Duration +90%, Effect +90%)-Kisara (Duration +20%)

The recipe is automatically obtained when Kisara and Dohalim join the team

Sandwich

Recipe : Sandwich\ Effect : Sacred mark (more difficult to be spotted by the enemies)\ Ingredient : -Wheat x2-Chicken x1-Lettuce x2-Tomato x1\ Favo-rite dish of : Kisara (Duration +20%)

The recipe is a reward of the side quest "The owl sanctuary" (Mahag Saar - Niez). Your answers do not matter, you will still get the recipe.

Hamburger

Recipe : Hamburger\ Effect : Elemental Defense +III (+20%)\ Ingredient : -Wheat x2-Lettuce x1-Tomato x2-Sheep meat x1 \ Favo-rite dish of : Law (Duration -25%, Effect +)

The recipe is in a chest in the Forland Mountains (Ganath Haros - South Hiking Trail), east of the central part of the area.

Omelette

Recipe : Omelette \ Effect : Defense +I (+10%)\ Ingredient : -Tomato x2-Egg x1 \ Favo-rite dish of : Kisara (Duration +20%)

The recipe is in a blue box in the library of the Palace of Autelina (Menancia), in the northwest.

Curry mabo

Recipe : Curry mabo \ Effect : Recovery of SP after combat II (15 SP) \ Ingredient :- Rice x3-Laporc meat x1-Chilli x2-Tofu x1 \ Favo-rite dish of : Alphen (Effect +15%)

The recipe is a reward for the side quest "The Gourmet Saga: Silky and Fluffy" (Ganath Haros - Level 2 - Pelegion). To access it, you must have completed the first two quests of the Gourmet Saga

Cheese fondue

Recipe : Cheese fondue \ Effect : Combat points bonus I \ Ingredient : -Wheat x2-Milk x1-Egg x1\ Favo-rite dish of : Shionne (Ingredients used x2, Duration +90%, Effect + 90%)

The recipe is obtained automatically once Dohalim joins the team.

Porridge

Recipe : Porridge \ Effect : Defence + \ Ingredient : Wheat x3\ Favo-rite dish of : Shionne (ingredients x2, effect +90%, duration +90%)

This is the starting recipe so you have it automatically

Porridge Murus Flegit

Recipe : Porridge Murus Flegit\ Effect : PS recovery after combat III (20 PS) \ Ingredient :- Rice x2-Chicken x1-Egg x1-Mushroom x2\ Favo-rite dish of : Shionne (Ingredients used x2, Duration +90%, Effect + 90%)

After getting the Shionne, Dohalim and Hootle pancake recipes, go camping and you will get the recipe

Location of people to be treated with Shionne
NPC N°1

Location: Rudhir Forest

On the bridge accessible via the scale on your map.
NPC N°2

Location: Cyslodia - Underground channel

NPC N°3

Location: Cyslodia - Frozen Valley

On the tree right next to the wooden bridge there is an owl giving the Half-Circles as well as a person to heal for Shionne giving 5 strawberries.

NPCS N°4 TO 6

Location: Menancia - Observation Center

On the way to the road to Traslida, the side quest "The healer and her patients" starts automatically. You have a campfire right next to it so don't be afraid to use your SPs to heal them. The first one will give you 2 Beast Tails, and the second one 5 eggs. The poet then appears a little further on and gives you 2 Mollusc Tentacles to finish the quest. This quest is part of the main story so you can't miss them.

NPC N°7

Location: Menancia - Traslida Road

Just below the bridge, in the center of the area.

NPC N°8

Location: Menancia - Plain of Tietal

In the southeast of the area, in the same place as the owl

NPC N°9

Location: Menancia - Talka Pond Road

In the middle of your path, after the campfire

NPC N°10

Location: Menancia - Mount Dhiara - Mountain Trail

At the northernmost ladder, then use the vines to descend and enter the cave

NPC N°11

Location: Menancia - Mount Dhiara - Mountain Trail

At the very southwest of the area, at the end of the road.

NPC N°12

Location: Maha Island - Lac d'Adan

In the house to the south.

NPC N°13

Location: Ganath Haros - Wood of the Shining Waterfall

It is the first one on the left when you arrive in the area.

NPC N°14

Location: Ganath Haros - Lavtu Swamp

NPC N°15

Location: Other - Lenegis - Residential Zone 16

NPC N°16

Location: Other - Daeq Faezol - Lower Level

Location of all Artifacts
CROCODILE CRUSHER

Name : Crocodile Crusher\ Effect : Artes' Panoply +1\ Location : Menancia - Mount Dhiara - Mountain Trail

Artifact obtained during the main adventure when arriving at the Mountain Path

LADY'S SHIELD

Name : Lady's shield \ Effect : Equipment transfer \ Location : Calaglia - Castle of Glanymede - throne room

Artifact obtained by finding the special owl n°33.

SHINING SPHERE

Name : Shining sphere\ Effect : Transfer of archives\ Location : Calaglia - Arid lands of Iglia

Artifact obtained by finding the special owl n°34

BROKEN MACHINE GUN

Name: BROKEN MACHINE GUN\ Effect : Transfer of money and objects \ Location : Cyslodia - Prison Tower of Riville - Secret room

Artifact obtained by finding the special owl n°35

OLD EXCAVATOR

Name: Old excavator \ Effect : Level transfer \ Location : Menancia - Autelina Palace - 2nd level - Guard Room

Artifact obtained by finding the special owl n°36.

MINER'S CAP

Name: Miner's cap \ Effect : Transfer of control of artes \ Location : Other - Uninhabited Island

Artifact obtained by finding the special owl n°37.

In order to access the Uninhabited Island, you must start the side quest "Beyond Death". To unlock it, you must have reached the final dungeon in Rena. Come back to the Tuah Shores (Ganath Haros). As soon as you enter the area, a scene will start where you find a bottle on the ground.

After that, go to the Secret Harbor (Mahag Saar) and show it to the one who drives the boat. You have now unlocked the access to the uninhabited island. Continue towards the green star, defeat the boss, and you can finally get the owl.

TRIDENT

Name: TRIDENT \ Effect : Transfer of skills \ Location : Ganath Haros - Del Fharis Castle - Lord's room

Artifact obtained by finding the special owl n°38.

MECHANICAL CREATURE

Name: Mechanical creature \ Effect : Transfer of outfits \ Location : Other - Owl Forest

Artifact obtained as a reward for finding the 38 owls and talking to the owl king to complete the quest

WOLVERINE CODE

Name: WOLVERINE CODE \ Effect : Refined cooking 2 (Recipe duration +20%) \ Location : Calaglia – Mosgul

Artifact obtained as a reward for the side quest "Globalization". This quest is only available after completing the side quest "The Gourmet Saga: Silky and Fluffy" (Ganath Haros - Pelegion - 2nd level).

LABYRINTH OF THE GLUTTON

Name: Labyrinth of the glutton \ Effect : Refined cuisine 1 (Recipe duration +10%) \ Location : Mahag Saar - Collines d'Aqfotle

This artifact is obtained as a reward for the side quest "The Gourmet Saga: Scent of the Meadows". To obtain this quest, you must have completed the first two quests of the Gourmet Saga in Cyslodia and Menancia.

WOLVERINE CODE

Name: WOLVERINE CODE \ Effect : Refined cooking 2 (Recipe duration +20%) \ Location : Calaglia – Mosgul

This artifact is obtained as a reward for the side quest "Globalization". This quest is only available after completing the side quest "The Gourmet's Saga: Soft and Silky" (Ganath Haros - Pelegion - Level 2).

WOLVERINE'S GUIDE

Name: WOLVERINE'S GUIDE \ Effect : Refined cuisine 3 (Recipe duration +80%) \ Location : Menancia - Autelina Palace - Library

Artifact obtained as a reward for the side quest "The Spectral Flower of Nevira" (Menancia - Snowy Plains of Nevira). This quest is only available after defeating the fifth lord. After that, go to the library of Autelina Palace to trigger a scene near the shelves. Then go to the Snowy Plains of Nevira and fight the level 54 monster (the fight can be quite difficult so be level 55 minimum to avoid difficulties). You will also get an Astral Flower

SILVER ARMOR

Name: SILVER ARMOR \ Effect : EXP bonus (+20%) \ Location : Ganth Haros - Temple de Saxleoh – Pelegion

This artifact is obtained as a reward for the side quest "Their Future" (Ganth Haros - Temple of Saxleoh - Pelegion). In order for the quest to be available, it is necessary to have healed the soldier on the Road to Talka Pond with Shionne.

GOLDEN ARMOR

Name: GOLDEN ARMOR \ Effect : Super EXP bonus (+80%) \ Location : Menancia - Traslida Road

This artifact is obtained as a reward for the side quest "Spiritual Temple". This quest becomes available only after defeating the fifth lord. When you do, go and trigger the quest by talking to the man near the campfire. This is a rather difficult quest so it is recommended to wait until you are level 60 - 65 to do it. You will have to go through a dungeon and then face an optional boss quite similar to Efrit Malum.

MASKED DEMON SKULL

Name: MASKED DEMON SKULL \ Effect : Perfect Carefree (+100% damage done and received) \ Location : Menancia - Viscint - Training ground

Reward for completing the Advanced version of the solo challenge with Dohalim.

SCULPTURE OF THE DEVIL

Name: SCULPTURE OF THE DEVIL \ Effect : Difficulty Chaos \ Location : Menancia - Viscint - Training ground

Reward for completing the Ultimate version of the Dohalim solo challenge.

SEALING BLADE

Name: SEALING BLADE \ Effect : Minimum damage\ Location : Mahag Island - Lac d'Adan

The artifact is in a chest at the Lake of Adan, in the tower at the very west of the area.

LUCKY CAT

Name: LUCKY CAT\ Effect : PC bonus (+20%) \ Location : Mahag Saar – Niez

Artifact obtained as a reward for the side quest "Echoes" (Mahag Saar - Niez). You will have to defeat the Giant Zeugle "Merciless".

LUCKY GOLD CAT

Name: LUCKY GOLD CAT\ Effect : Super PC bonus (+80%) \ Location : Ganath Haros - Aureum Waterfalls - Upper Level – Exit

This artifact is obtained as a reward for the side quest "A Mad Rage" (Ganath Haros - Thistlym). You will have to go through an optional area and defeat a hidden boss to get the recipe. Near the camp of the Shining Waterfall Woods, you will find a corner of water where you can swim and enter a new area. Do the dungeon, beat the boss and finish the quest. Be around level 57 because the boss is not especially difficult but has two stages.

DRUM OF HELL

Name: DRUM OF HELL\ Effect : Combat points bonus (+20%) \ Location : Ganath Haros - Aureum Waterfalls - Upper Level – Exit

This artifact is in a chest in the Aureum Waterfalls. To reach it, from the Exit on the upper level, you have the choice between two paths: the one on the right consists in jumping into the void and going down the whole waterfall to get 1 red Rosemary. Don't worry, a ladder allows you to go back up very quickly and you will find the artifact at the top.

TOP DRUM

Name: TOP DRUM\ Effect : Super battle point bonus (+80%) \ Location : Mahag Saar – Niez

This artifact is obtained as a reward for the side quest "Farewell, dear mage" (Mahag Saar - Niez). This quest can only be obtained after completing the quest "Echoes" given by the same person. This quest will take you to the very top of Mount Dhiara: be at least level 65, because the fight there against Sylph Procella is difficult.

FLICKERING CANDLES

Name: FLICKERING CANDLES \ Effect : Abundant ore \ Location : Mahag Saar – Niez

This artifact is obtained as a reward for the side quest "The Unlikely Duo". Since this quest is given by the Golden Voice, you must have finished the side quest "A Healer and Her Patients" (Menancia - Observation Center) first.

The object you are looking for is the Iron Pipe""", is located in the very north of the Arid Lands of Iglia (Calaglia)

GOLDEN FAIRY STATUE

Name: GOLDEN FAIRY STATUE\ Effect : Abundant ore\ Location : Cyslodia - Cysloden - Avenue de la place de la fontaine

This artifact is obtained as a reward for the side quests "A Perfect World" and "Lesson in Humility". To unlock these two quests, you will have to complete the four side quests consisting of defeating the optional bosses representing an element. Then you will only have to watch the two scenes to get the artifact.

MECHANICAL DOLL

Name: MECHANICAL DOLL \ Effect : Makes you invisible \ Location : Other - The Otherworld - Land of Judgment

To get this artifact, you will have to complete the bonus dungeon and beat "Chronos" (level 95) at the end. To unlock this dungeon, it is necessary to finish the following side quests (Menancia - Traslida Road):

-Spiritual Temple

-A strange atmosphere

-Visitors from another world

Fishing: how does it work?

Before you rush out and throw the bait at random when you find a new pond, first take the time to press Triangle / Y to bring up the list of available fish in the pond and the rod and bait currently in use.

The first thing to do to ensure you get the fish you want is to use the right bait. This is because each bait has an "Easy Catch", meaning that if the fish is in the pond and you use a bait that is an Easy Catch, there is a good chance that it will be that particular fish that takes the bait. For example, let's say we want to get a Talka Trout. We'll use the Celestial Whale bait to greatly increase our chances that the fish that takes the hook will be a Talka Trout, not one of the other fish available in the pond.

The second thing to consider is the combination to enter when you throw the hook. Next to the name of each fish is a combination of two buttons (for example, Cross; Cross). If you want a particular fish, you must not only choose the right bait, but also enter the right combination. Again using the example of the Talka Trout, you would enter Triangle; Square (Y; X). By combining the two elements (the bait and the button combination), you can be almost certain that the fish biting on the hook will be the one you want. Cast your bait in an area where you have seen a fish (the circle turns yellow), enter the combination several times until the fish bites, and, once it does, the mini-game really begins

Once the fish has bitten, two life bars appear: yours and the fish's. To lower the fish's life bar, simply press the right keys at the right time (R1, R2, L1 or left stick in the right direction). You will catch the fish once its life bar is completely empty. However, if your life bar ever touches the right edge in the red, the fish will run away. This bar tends to turn a little green each time you succeed in the QTEs, but it tends to turn strongly red each time you make a mistake, which usually doesn't leave you much room for error (2 - 3 times, especially if they are consecutive mistakes).

Some fish, called legendary fish, have two life bars and are more difficult to catch. In general, and especially if you are only fishing for trophies/achievements (consisting of catching all types of fish), wait until you finish the Ultimate Solo Fight with Kisara to get the Navy Rod. This rod allows you to catch all fish and avoids the headache of knowing which rod can catch which fish. With this rod, those fish won't really be a problem for you anymore.

Where to find all the lures and rods ?

THE LEURRES

Name of the lure	How to obtain	Location
Beginner's popper	Fishing expert reward for catching 1 fish	Talka Pond Road
Marine float	Fishing expert award for catching 25 different fish	Talka Pond Road
Round popper	Fishing expert award for catching 15 different fish	Talka Pond Road
Teepo lure	Fishing expert award for catching 35 different fish	Talka Pond Road
Stick lure	Chest (Lavtu Swamp)	-
Bienfu lure	Trunk (Forland Mountains - South Hiking Trail)	-

Surface Mirage	Chest (Ruins of Adan)	-
Elegant swimmer	Fishing expert award for catching 3 different fish	Talka Pond Road
Disarming lure	Purchase from the inn's merchant	Cysloden
	Reward Novice solo combat with Kisara	Training ground
Minnow laporc	Reward for the side quest "Like two drops of water".	Cysloden
Thunder lure	Purchase from the inn's merchant	Viscint
Charming lure	Purchase from the inn's merchant	Deny
Zapie's look-alike	Chest (Fogwharl limestone caves)	
Mud slider	Fishing expert award for catching 5 different fish	Talka Pond Road
Rock tapper	Purchase from the inn's merchant	Pelegion
Good Lead	Reward Advanced solo combat with Kisara	Training ground
Tapping device	Chest (Lake Adan)	-
Super rotator	Fishing expert award for catching 30 different fish	Talka Pond Road
Silver croc lure	Fishing expert award for catching 40 different fish	Talka Pond Road

FISHING RODS

Name of the cane	How to obtain	Location
Navy cane	Ultimate Solo Combat Reward with Kisara	Training ground
Beginner's material	Fishing expert award for catching 10 different fish	Talka Pond Road
Ambush fisherman	Fishing expert award for catching 20 different fish	Talka Pond Road
Tenebrae Mk III	Fishing expert award for catching 44 different fish	Talka Pond Road
Cane of Migal	Starting cane	-

Liste et localisation de tous les poissons

If you need a lure to catch your fish, you can find the location of all the lures and rods in the game here.

CALAGLIA - CAVE OF SOLITUDE

Fish	Combination	Lure
Cave bar	SQUARE CROSS / X A	Marine float
Amber mackerel	TRIANGLE TRIANGLE / Y Y	Tapping device
Flatfish coral	TRIANGLE SQUARE / Y X	Elegant swimmer
Karasuba sea bream	CROSS TRIANGLE / A Y	Marine float
Salmon of Lacerda	TRIANGLE TRIANGLE / Y Y	Surface Mirage

CYSLODIA - SNOWY PLAINS OF NEVIRA

Fish	Combination	Lure
Tilapia of pond	CROSS TRIANGLE / A Y	Surface Mirage
Rabid Piranha	TRIANGLE CROSS / Y A	Tapping device
Tricolored catfish	SQUARE CROSS / A X	Mud slider
Polar bar	CROSS TRIANGLE / A Y	Rock tapper
Piranha of Nevira	CROSS CROSS / A A	Disarming lure
Armored sturgeon	SQUARE TRIANGLE / X Y	Better lead

CYSLODIA - FROZEN VALLEY

Fish	Combination	Lure
Hawksbill Trout	TRIANGLE CROSS / Y A	Thunder lure
Pearl Pike	SQUARE TRIANGLE / X Y	Super rotator
Polar bar	CROSS TRIANGLE / A Y	Rock tapper
Azure Tilapia	CROSS CROSS / A A	Disarming lure
Cyslodia Salmon	SQUARE CROSS / A X	Super rotator

MENANCIA - OBSERVATION CENTER

Fish	Combination	Lure
Tilapia of pond	CROSS TRIANGLE / A Y	Surface Mirage
Rabid Piranha	TRIANGLE CROSS / Y A	Tapping device
Hawksbill Trout	TRIANGLE CROSS / Y A	Thunder lure
Bar de la Menancia	SQUARE CROSS / A X	Thunder lure
Arowana of Traslida	SQUARE CROSS / A X	Stick lure

Golden catfish	TRIANGLE CROSS / Y A	Beneficial lure

MENANCIA - TALKA POND ROAD

Fish	Combination	Lure
Dahna Bar	CROSS CROSS / A A	Beginner's popper
Tilapia of pond	CROSS TRIANGLE / A Y	Surface Mirage
Hawksbill Trout	TRIANGLE CROSS / Y A	Thunder lure
Catfish from Menancia	SQUARE CROSS / A X	Round popper
Talka trout	TRIANGLE SQUARE / Y X	Celestial whale

MAHAG SAAR - LAKE ADAN

Fish	Combination	Lure
Dahna Bar	CROSS CROSS / A A	Beginner's popper
Rabid Piranha	TRIANGLE CROSS / Y A	Tapping device
Tricolored catfish	SQUARE CROSS / A X	Mud slider
Azure Tilapia	CROSS CROSS / A A	Disarming lure
Pirarucu of vase	SQUARE CROSS / A X	Charming lure
Arowana from Aureum	SQUARE CROSS / A X	Teepo lure

MAHAG SAAR - ADAN RUINS

Fish	Combination	Lure
Hawksbill Trout	TRIANGLE CROSS / Y A	Thunder lure
Cave bar	SQUARE CROSS / X A	Marine float
Emerald salmon	TRIANGLE TRIANGLE / Y Y	Thunder lure
Small pirarucu	SQUARE CROSS / A X	Charming lure
Arowana of Aqfotle	SQUARE TRIANGLE / X Y	Stick lure

MAHAG SAAR - SECRET PORT

Fish	Combination	Lure
Vesper bar	SQUARE CROSS / X A	Marine float
Sardonyx Grouper	SQUARE TRIANGLE / X Y	Surface Mirage
Garnet sea bream	CROSS TRIANGLE // A Y	Disarming lure
Red tuna	TRIANGLE SQUARE / Y X	Celestial whale
Barracuda of the Mahag Saar	CROSS CROSS / A A	Super rotator

Silver marlin	SQUARE CROSS / X A	Silver croc lure

GANATH HAROS - WOOD OF THE BRIGHT WATERFALL

Fish	Combination	Lure
Dahna Bar	CROSS CROSS / A A	Beginner's popper
Piranha of Ganath Haros	TRIANGLE CROSS / Y A	Stick lure
Tricolored catfish	SQUARE CROSS / A X	Mud slider
Catfish - Ganath Haros	SQUARE CROSS / A X	Round popper
Green Pike	CROSS TRIANGLE / A Y	Rock tapper

GANATH HAROS - LAVTU SWAMP

Fish	Combination	Lure
Dahna Bar	CROSS CROSS / A A	Beginner's popper
Tilapia of Lavtu	TRIANGLE TRIANGLE / Y Y	Celestial whale
Tricolored catfish	SQUARE CROSS / A X	Mud slider
Arowana by Lavtu	SQUARE CROSS / A X	Rock tapper
Small pirarucu	SQUARE CROSS / A X	Charming lure
Cobalt trout	TRIANGLE SQUARE / Y X	Minnow laporc

GANATH HAROS - FOGWHARL LIMESTONE CAVES

Fish	Combination	Lure
Piranha of Ganath Haros	TRIANGLE CROSS / Y A	Stick lure
Pearl Pike	SQUARE TRIANGLE / X Y	Super rotator
Azure Tilapia	CROSS CROSS / A A	Disarming lure
Catfish - Ganath Haros	SQUARE CROSS / A X	Round popper
Fogwharl's Pike	CROSS TRIANGLE / A Y	Mud slider
Pirarucu swan	CROSS TRIANGLE / A Y	Zapie's look-alike

OTHER - UNINHABITED ISLAND

Fish	Combination	Lure
Vesper bar	SQUARE CROSS / X A	Marine float
Tsuyukusa mackerel	TRIANGLE TRIANGLE / Y Y	Tapping device

Mahag Saa flatfish	TRIANGLE SQUARE / Y X	Charming lure
Spiny Grouper	SQUARE TRIANGLE / X Y	Round popper
Gluttonous Barracuda	CROSS CROSS / A A	Elegant swimmer

The ranch: How to raise livestock efficiently?

The ranch is unlocked by doing the side quest "Pharia's Ranch". You can't really miss it since Bogdel is in the middle of the road. Go back to his farm to complete the quest and unlock the ranch.

First, let's look at the livestock that can be raised. There are a total of six different animals: Cow, Pig, Chicken, Horse, Sheep and Slider. Each animal has different characteristics that will influence the result and therefore the amount of meat you get. For example, the progress for a cow will be very slow while that of a chicken will be much faster so if you start raising cows and chickens at the same time, the chicken will be ready much faster.

However, there are outside elements that can interfere with the growth of your livestock. These elements are directly related to the type of livestock in the barn. For example, if you put pigs in the barn, they will attract Zeugles, which will kill your livestock (pigs and other animals). Similarly, mice can slow down the growth of livestock (but not stop it)

Thus, avoiding Zeugles attacks should be a priority when raising livestock. To do this, you have two options: put guard dogs, or add horses to the barn that have the ability to repel Zeugles. For example, let's say you want to get pig meat. If you put only pigs in the barn, even with two guard dogs, your yields will be lower because they will attract Zeugles a lot, and most will die. It is much better to place only four pigs and one horse in the barn to avoid losing your livestock at all costs. This way, even if you put less pigs in the barn, you will get more meat because there were no attacks.

Before confirming the placement of an animal in the barn, you will have the opportunity to choose the animal's diet

Obviously, miracle food is the best food because it accelerates growth and the number of meat per animal. But it also costs twice as much. So it's up to you to decide if you are willing to invest the money, or if you prefer to be more patient and save your money. If you have several animals in your barn, but only one particular animal is your priority, you might as well give miracle food to that animal, and conventional food to the others in order to limit costs.

Last detail, the basic time to get meat from a normal growing animal, with free food, which has not suffered from mouse attack, is half an hour in game time, not in real time. For fast-growing livestock with fast or miracle food, this time can be reduced to ten minutes. For mice that can slow down the growth of your cattle, if you go to your ranch at night when there are cattle there, you can help your cats chase the mice away. Examine the mice to get them to leave and avoid stunting the growth of your animals.

To summarize, be careful with the animals in the barn so you don't attract too many Zeugles, always have at least one cat and one dog on guard (there's no reason to take them off guard), feed miracle food to the livestock you're interested in, and you'll have all the meat you need to cook the most powerful dishes. Law also unlocks the title "Friend of the Beasts" once you've raised all six types of livestock available.

Goldsmithing: How to make the most powerful accessories?

MANUFACTURING OF ACCESSORIES

In order to make an accessory, all you need is the right materials. You will always need only one material to make a prop. Each item has a basic effect that will always be the same. For example, the Poison Charm will always have poison immunity, the Magic Emblem will have elemental attack

+15% etc.

However, where you can create unique accessories, and thus where the whole crafting system of the game comes into its own, is in the next step, when you will choose, among all the materials you have, which one you will use, as they all have different effects that will allow you to adjust your accessory to your needs. So, using the example in the screenshot above, creating a Magic Emblem only requires 1 Astral Ore: out of the 52 I have, all 52 have additional effects that can be added to the effect of the basic accessory (Elemental Attack +15%), and you have to choose the one that brings the most interesting side effects to create the accessory that best suits your needs. As you can see from the screenshots below, there are many different possibilities depending on the ore used, so you should take the time to look at all the possibilities.

The number of additional skills you will have on your accessory in addition to the main skill depends directly on the rarity of the ore used (the small colored number indicated on the ore). An ore of rarity 1 adds no additional skill, the one of rank 2 adds 1, the one of rank 3 adds 2, the one of rank 4 adds 3, and finally the one of rank 5 adds 4. So, the more you use a rare mineral, the more powerful an accessory you can create since it will have more additional skills. Please note that the rarity of the ore depends directly on your progress in the game, and not on the place where you find it. Indeed, once the main story is over, it will be quite possible to find rank 5 ore in the very first areas of the game for example, even if these sources will be less likely to give this kind of rarity than the sources at the end of the game.

THE TRANSFER OF COMPETENCE

Once you have made your prop, you can make it even more powerful by adjusting the additional skills through skill transfer. To do this, you'll need to create another item with an additional skill that you want to have on the first item you made. For example, let's say we want to accumulate the light damage bonus on our Magic Emblem accessory which already has an additional skill "Light Damage +15%". Let's create another accessory with the additional skill "Light Damage +15%" (it's important that it's an additional skill, otherwise you won't be able to transfer it).

In order to transfer the additional skill "Light Damage +15" from Curse Charm, you will have to raise the accessory to the maximum level. You can only transfer a skill if the item is at its maximum level. To level up an accessory, use useless ores, whose additional skills you are not interested in. Rank 1 ores are perfect for upgrading items since they have no additional skills. In general, try to make your prop to upgrade (or the skill you are interested in) at a low level (2 or 3 ideally) so that you don't use too many ores for leveling up.

Once you have reached the right level, you can finally use skill transfer and pass the skill onto your target prop. So, to create overpowered accessories, you have to create a first accessory with rank 5 (or the highest rank you can), then create other accessories with a lower rank whose additional skills you are interested in so that you can transfer them on your main accessory and cumulate the most effect possible. Be careful though, once the skill is transferred, the accessory whose skill you take will disappear permanently.

It is through this process of skill transfer between props that you can create props that fit your exact needs and can trivialize a fight that was previously a big problem. The easiest way to take advantage of this system is to stack the same effect multiple times. This is especially effective against bosses who use only one element: you can simply stack resistances against that element and ignore most attacks. You can also make the opposite choice and accumulate the damage of an element to exploit its weakness.

How to get all the Astral Flowers?

BEAT ALL THE GIANT ZEUGLES

The first step to getting all the Astral Flowers is to find and defeat the 20 Giant Zeugles found throughout the different areas. Each Giant Zeugle allows you to get 1 Flower after your victory. You can find here the location and a video of the fight for each Giant Zeugle.

FINISH THE SIDE QUEST "BEYOND DEATH

An Astral Flower is obtained by completing the Beyond Death side quest.

In order to access the Uninhabited Island, you must start the side quest "Beyond Death". To unlock it, you must have reached the final dungeon in Rena. Come back to the Tuah Shores (Ganath Haros). As soon as you enter the area, a scene will start where you find a bottle on the ground

After that, go to the Secret Harbor (Mahag Saar) and show it to the one who drives the boat. You have now unlocked the access to the Uninhabited Island. Continue towards the green star and defeat the boss to complete the quest

COMPLETE THE ULTIMATE TEAM FIGHT CHALLENGE

The last ten Astral Flowers are obtained by completing the Ultimate Team Fight challenge (recommended level 99), where you will have to beat a copy-paste of the Giant Zeugle Dancer of Death. The main difficulty of the fight is that in the Training Ground you can't use any items. This makes Shionne and/or Dohalim more or less indispensable.

That being said, with the right equipment and strategy, this fight can be completed at much lower levels (around level 80) on Normal difficulty. Since the boss is weak to Light, take the opportunity to force Shionne and Rinwell to use only Light Artes by discarding all other Artes.

To further capitalize on the boss's weakness, make accessories with additional skills to increase light damage. The more you cumulate them, the better it will be. So, as long as Shionne and Dohalim don't get knocked out (at the same time), not being able to use an item shouldn't be a problem.

Manufacture all weapons

In Tales of Arise, you will have to craft 100 weapons to get the "Armed to the teeth" trophy / achievement (out of 103 possible). Here are all the weapons to craft for each character, and where to find the necessary materials.

ALPHEN

Long sword

Materials : Sharp Fang x2 / Enemies to farmer : Bee, Wolf, Ice wolf, Alpha ice wolf, Falcon, Berserker

Rough sword

Materials	Enemies to farmer
Solid bone *x8*	Armadillo, Ice Wolf, Alpha Ice Wolf, Deceptive Effigy
Spherical shell x2	Armadillo
Astral Crystal Grain x1	Can only be found in safes

Croc terrien

Materials	Enemies to farmer
Sharp Fang x6	Bee, Wolf, Ice wolf, Alpha ice wolf, Falcon,

	Berserker
Earth seed x2	Montitentacule, Montitentacule of the woods

Storm wing

Materials	Enemies to farmer
Solid bone x8	Tatou, Loup des glaces, Loup des glaces Alpha, Effigie trompeuse
Mane of beast x2	Alpha atrophied wolf
Sharp pen x1	Falcon

Lightning tooth

Materials	Enemies to farmer
Giant Sharp Fang x4	Assault bee, Atrophied wolf, Scaled wolf, Archer falcon, Clawed rifleman, Boar, Unleashed boar, Vandal dragon, Bug, Unleashed bug
Mollusc tentacle x1	Mollusc with propulsion
Granite hook x1	Wild boar

Fire Claw

Materials	Enemies to farmer
Giant Sharp Fang x6	Assault bee, Atrophied wolf, Scaled wolf, Archer falcon, Clawed rifleman, Boar, Unleashed boar, Vandal dragon, Bug, Unleashed bug
Titanium cuff x2	Monkey

Ultra Storm Wing

Materials	Enemies to farmer
Giant Sharp Fang x3	Assault bee, Atrophied wolf, Scaled wolf, Archer falcon, Clawed rifleman, Boar, Unleashed boar, Vandal dragon, Bug, Unleashed bug
Thunderstorm spout x2	Archer Falcon
Storm wing	-

Croc terrien ultra

Materials	Enemies to farmer
Mega rigid bone x4	Armadillo shredder, Precious armadillo, Atrophied wolf, Alpha atrophied wolf, Clawed emu, Monkey, Fatal effigy, Propelled mollusk, Moss shell
Windy mane x2	Atrophied wolf, Alpha atrophied wolf, Scaled wolf, Alpha scaled wolf
Croc terrien	-

Aurum Long Sword

Materials	Enemies to farmer
Giant Sharp Fang x4	Assault bee, Atrophied wolf, Scaled wolf, Archer falcon, Clawed rifleman, Boar, Unleashed boar, Vandal dragon, Bug, Unleashed bug
Hard spherical shell x2	Tatou déchiqueteur, Tatou compresseur, Tatou précieux
Long sword	-

Ultra Fire Claw

Materials	Enemies to farmer
Giant Sharp Fang x2	Assault bee, Atrophied wolf, Scaled wolf, Archer falcon, Clawed rifleman, Boar, Unleashed boar, Vandal dragon, Bug, Unleashed bug
Ice Fang x2	Wild Boar
Fire Claw	-

Ultra lightning tooth

Materials	Enemies to farmer
Giant Sharp Fang x3	Assault bee, Atrophied wolf, Scaled wolf, Archer falcon, Clawed rifleman, Boar, Unleashed boar, Vandal dragon, Bug, Unleashed bug
Sticky tentacle x2	Foam shell
Lightning tooth	-

Solid blade

Materials	Enemies to farmer
Giant Sharp Fang x8	Assault bee, Atrophied wolf, Scaled wolf, Archer falcon, Clawed rifleman, Boar, Unleashed boar, Vandal dragon, Bug, Unleashed bug Helganquil
Bright astral crystal x1	Helganquil

Supreme lightning tooth

Materials	Enemies to farmer
Tearing titan fang x2	Exceptional Bee, Prismabeille, Fortified Wolf, Fortified Wolf alpha, Livid Wolf, Livid Wolf alpha, Hunter Wolf, Hunter Wolf alpha, Snow Wolf, Snow Wolf alpha, Astral Famine, Sylph Feather, Garuglace, Rapayon, Double-bladed, Fortified Disintegrator, Eradicator, Fiery Boar, Astral Isolation, Fiery Dragon, Polycontrus, Figure of Immortality, Tearing Titan

	Beast, Astral Sloth, Scabby Beasts
Sticky tentacle x2	Foam shell
Ultra lightning tooth	-

Supreme Storm Wing

Materials	Enemies to farmer
Tearing titan fang x2	Exceptional Bee, Prismabeille, Fortified Wolf, Fortified Wolf alpha, Livid Wolf, Livid Wolf alpha, Hunter Wolf, Hunter Wolf alpha, Snow Wolf, Snow Wolf alpha, Astral Famine, Sylph Feather, Garuglace, Rapayon, Double-bladed, Fortified Disintegrator, Eradicator, Fiery Boar, Astral Isolation, Fiery Dragon, Polycontrus, Figure of Immortality, Tearing Titan Beast, Astral Sloth, Scabby Beasts
Stormy Fang x2	Polymentus
Ultra Storm Wing	-

Carrot machete

Materials	Enemies to farmer
Dark mane x6	Fortified wolf, Fortified wolf alpha, Livid wolf, Livid wolf alpha, Hunter wolf, Hunter wolf alpha, Snow wolf, Snow wolf alpha
Fragment of ganit x2	Magmalem, Guardian Gnome, Magma Golem
Ossified stem	Montitentacule in flower

.....

Farmer the Exp to reach level 100

In Tales of Arise, the "Apogee" trophy/achievement requires reaching level 100 with your team. Although this may seem like a long time, fortunately there are many elements that make it much easier

First of all, once the main story is over, finish the side quest "Spiritual Temple" (Menancia -Traslida Road). Thanks to this quest, you will get as a reward the artifact Golden Armor allowing to get +80% EXP after each fight. Also take the time to do the side quest "Their Future" (Ganath Haros - Pelegion - Temple of Saxleoh) to get the Silver Armor artifact to get +20% EXP as well.

Now you will have to do the side quest "A strange atmosphere" given by a woman at the entrance of Viscint. This quest is simply to return to the Temple of the Spirit and the Earth and allows you to unlock the quest we are interested in: "Visitors from another world".

This quest is the traditional quest that allows other characters from the old games of the series to come and rub shoulders with the cast of the current game. You will have to fight a series of bosses from the old Tales of in order to complete this quest. When you start it, you will probably be around level 60. Continue through the dungeon until you reach the last boss and you should naturally reach level 80 (this mostly depends on the difficulty you chose: if you play Hard or Chaos, you'll probably be level 90 while if you play Story mode, you can reach it as early as level 75). You can check out our guide to all the bosses in this quest if you want more information on how to get past a particular boss.

The goal of the method is to farm the end boss of the dungeon, Chronos, which you can face as many times as you want. Before you face him, go and cook Sushi with Dohalim to receive +30% extra EXP once the duration of the dish has been halved. Also, buy lots of jellies to restore your HP so you don't have to go back and forth each time and can restart the fight right away.

If the fight is too difficult for your level, you can simply set the difficulty to Story mode and it shouldn't really be a problem anymore. Beating him once will get you Nebilim, Alphen's infernal weapon. If you've used Alphen a lot during the story, chances are it's your most powerful weapon so it can help you get through the fight more easily. You can also farm EXP on enemies in the dungeon until you are stronger, especially from the Scarlet Night Rift, which yields a lot of EXP per battle.

Stuffing herbs to improve statistics

In Tales of Arise, you will find herbs throughout your adventure that can improve your characters' stats. If these herbs do not grow back after being collected, they can still be farmed thanks to the Viscint Training Ground.

In the Training Ground (Viscint - Menancia), you will find in the "Team Fighting" section, two challenges that are there exclusively to allow you to farm herbs that improve stats:

-Offensive medicinal herbs

-Defensive medicinal herbs

The only constraint is that you have to wait one hour before you can do these challenges again (1 hour in game time, not in real time, so you can't change the time zone to try to cheat the game). That's why, in order to get the most out of your time and these challenges, you should not hesitate to come and have a look around every hour while you progress in the adventure or while you do side quests. These challenges can be completed as soon as you arrive in Viscint. While they might be too difficult at first, they become much more affordable if you come in around level 35 - 40, especially if you switch the difficulty to Story mode.

If you start early enough, and come back to do the challenges regularly, you can get much higher stats than you're supposed to. That being said, since this is a long term farm, it's best to use the same herb on the same character every time to get the most out of it.

Visitors from another world

Edna

In Tales of Arise, one of the latest side quests that can be completed is the "Visitors from Another World" quest. This quest is the traditional quest that allows other characters from the old games of the series to come and play with the cast of the current game. You will have to fight a series of bosses from the old Tales of in order to finish this quest. Here is a detailed guide to the fight against Edna.

Boss : Edna / Level :63/ Weakness : Air/ Recommended level : 50 - 60 depending on the chosen difficulty

First remark, Edna has a weakness to wind: don't hesitate to exploit it, it's quite rare to be able to take advantage of bosses with weaknesses at this stage of the game and all of your characters are able, in one way or another, to use wind attacks. Conversely, do not use Earth Artes.

Second, Edna uses elemental attacks exclusively. This is a boon because it allows you to cook a hamburger right before the fight. If you cook it with Law, whose favorite food it is, you can boost the effect by 50% on a dish that already provides +20% elemental defense. Thanks to this, most of Edna's attacks become much less dangerous. You can even take it a step further by using elemental damage reducing accessories.

As for the combat itself, Edna often uses spells, allowing you to knock her down with Rinwell while she charges her Artes. Also, the only real physical attack she can perform is a charge with her umbrella that you can counter with Kisara. Including Alphen, that's three characters who have the opportunity to take her down. When this happens, take control of Alphen, sacrifice as much HP as you can, and do huge damage in one hit. By the way, avoid sticking to her because you won't be able to predict her attacks which are quite sudden, especially her charge with the umbrella. Put a few blows and then move away.

When Edna is about to launch her mystical Arte, the problems begin: she flies away and becomes more or less untouchable for the physical characters because she is much too mobile. Just dodge all the projectiles she throws at you and let your mages do some damage in the meantime. Fortunately, her mystical Shooting Star Arte (which is exactly the same spell Rinwell uses) is very easy to dodge: stay as far away from her as possible and you'll never get hit.

If you manage to survive this phase, the fight is the same until the end, so continue your strategy until you get through Edna.

Original Nimus

Boss : Original Nimus / Level :69/ Weakness : -/ Recommended level : 55 - 65 depending on the chosen difficulty

The original Nimus is simply a "reskin" of Valclynimus, except that now he has no weaknesses and has turned into a PV bag. In fact, the fight is exactly the same as the one you did in the last arc of the main adventure. So, apart from the fact that spamming the Artes of Light is no longer a viable strategy, you can do exactly the same thing again without any worries.

For the vast majority of the fight, the boss will just stand in the middle and let you hit him, occasionally defending himself without doing anything dangerous. However, sometimes he will jump and fall violently, letting waves escape on the ground. When he jumps, start hammering the dodge button: if you've learned the skills that facilitate perfect dodges, chances are you'll get one without a problem, allowing you not only to dodge the attack, but also to do some damage.

The easiest way to defeat this boss is simply to use Alphen's Bonus Strike to take down the boss. When he does, sacrifice your entire life bar and decimate his. He stays down so long that Shionne will have all the time in the world to heal you. Repeating this strategy is probably the easiest and most effective way to bring him back to the ground, which is important because otherwise you'll have trouble doing significant damage. You can also try to inflict Curse status with Shionne so that he takes double damage and speeds up the fight.

Vasneiys, Maleyis & Dulneiys

Boss	Level	Weakness	Recommended level
Vasneiys	75	Water	65-75
Maleyis	75	Darkness	65-75

Dulneiys	75	Lights	65-75

What's worse than a "colorswap" of an old boss than three colorswaps and having to face them at the same time. This fight is the same fight as the one against Meneiys you faced in the side quest "Nevira's Spectral Flower", except that it has been cut into three. Indeed, each boss has a part of the attacks of the original Meneiys.

The beginning of the fight will be by far the hardest part of the fight, especially when one of them will enter Out of Bounds. To get through this, focus on one at a time. The best way is to try to isolate one of them from the other two so that the fight is not too chaotic. To do this, set your strategies so that there is a "Stay away from enemies" action somewhere. This way, since there are three bosses, your allies will run away all the time and the bosses will chase them. So you can take the opportunity to take them apart in one-on-one. Since you are attacking him, you will have no problem getting his attention. Isolate the one who is causing you the most problems to make the rest of the fight much easier, and make sure you exploit his basic weaknesses.

This fight may be very long so avoid taking Law in the team because his fragility may make him die often. On the other hand, Kisara can be a good way to attract attention and separate into two groups. Finally, Shionne is a very good way to do damage while keeping some distance since she can attack from a distance without needing to take the time to charge an Arte. When you finally manage to kill one, the fight will become much easier, and more or less in the bag when there is only one left. The only thing that could be a problem is the lack of resources, so make sure that you don't waste too much of them during the fight.

Eizen

Boss : Eizen / Level :81/ Weakness : Air/ Recommended level : 70 - 75 depending on the chosen difficulty

Even if Eizen's attacks are different, the fight is quite similar to the one against Edna. Indeed, he also has a weakness to Wind, a resistance to Earth, and above all uses only elemental attacks. In fact, it is possible to reapply the same strategy as against his little sister, i.e. to have as much elemental defense as possible by cooking a hamburger and having accessories for this purpose. In this way, most of her attacks become harmless.

Unlike his little sister, Eizen is much more predictable: indeed, he tends to chain together three physical Elemental Artes (i.e. not spells) before stopping and giving you time to attack him. So you can simply dodge his attacks while your mages bombard him with wind attacks, then go on the offensive when he stops.

Eizen also has the ability to cast spells: this is your opportunity to knock him down with Rinwell. Take advantage of this opportunity to sacrifice as many HP as possible with Alphen and do huge damage.

Finally, Eizen's mystical Arte is, like his little sister's, quite easy to dodge and therefore not really dangerous. The latter will make charges on the ground which will cause waves of darkness that you can easily avoid by jumping provided that you are far enough away from him not to get hit when he runs at you.

Eizen & Edna

Boss : Eizen & Edna / Level :87/ Weakness : Air/ Recommended level :75-80

Again, the strategy you used to defeat Edna and then Eizen is still valid even when they are both: cook a hamburger just before the fight. If you cook it with Law, whose favorite food it is, you can boost the effect by 50% on a dish that already provides +20% elemental defense. Thanks to this, most of Edna and Eizen's attacks become much less dangerous. You can even take it a step further by using elemental damage reducing accessories.

When you have the opportunity to perform Bonus Hits to take them down, whether with Alphen or Rinwell, try to group them together to take them down at the same time and, more importantly, be able to deal huge damage to both at the same time with Alphen sacrificing as much HP as possible. Don't forget that Kisara's Bonus Strike can also block the charge with Edna's Umbrella.

Try to focus on only one at a time so that both can't enter Out of Bounds (which are identical) at the same time. Edna is much more fragile (and dangerous) than Eizen so focus on her at first. Once alone, Eizen will not be able to do much.

Chronos

Boss : Chronos / Level :95/ Weakness : -/ Recommended level : 80 - 90 depending on the chosen difficulty

Finally, you are facing the ultimate boss of the dungeon. While not to be underestimated, you've probably been through much worse to get this far. Chronos always seems to prioritize the character you control. This is the perfect opportunity to place three mages (Dohalim, Shionne and Rinwell) to bombard him while you face him one-on-one.

His attacks are very phony, especially the big laser he shoots in front of him: try to make sure that this laser does not go in the direction of your allies.

Moreover, don't stick to him because, on the one hand, you won't have time to react to his sharp blows, but more importantly, because he has the ability to surround himself with a magnetic field that will hurt you badly.

When he has lost half his life, Chronos can now use his Mystic Arte. This is a very easy attack to avoid since you only have to spin around so the laser doesn't hit you. Don't worry about your teammates, the AI is smart enough to dodge around and not get hit.

However, that's not the only thing that's new when he loses half his HP. Indeed, he now has an attack that allows him to stop time, and you can't do anything for almost ten seconds (not even pausing), leaving him the possibility to kill all your characters one by one without any resistance.

Fortunately, there are several solutions. First, you can try to stall him to prevent your team from being decimated in a few seconds. To do this, you need to make sure that everyone is at full health. You can also use Kisara's Bonus Strike just before to increase your defense. The longer it takes to kill someone, the fewer people it will kill, giving you a chance to get back into the fight.

But it gets even better, as there is a technique that allows you to completely ignore this phase... as long as your timing is right. Indeed, you may have noticed that when you use a Bonus Strike, no matter what the character is, he gains a short period of invincibility (about a second or two, the time it takes to go through an attack during the animation). The technique is to use a Bonus Hit just before he freezes time. In this way, you will find yourself frozen in a period of invincibility. However, since Chronos tends to target the player, he will try in vain to kill you, which completely cancels his attack.

Thanks to this, you will be able to ignore one of the biggest difficulties of the fight and defeat Chronos without too much trouble.

Infernal weapons : What are they for and how to farm the kills ?
HOW TO GET THE INFERNAL WEAPONS?

To get the infernal weapons you will have to defeat all the bosses in the side quest "Visitors from another world". This quest is only available after you have completed the side quest "A Strange Atmosphere" (Menancia - Viscint) in the Temple of the Earth Spirit, where a new NPC will have appeared

This quest is the traditional quest that allows other characters from the old games in the series to come and compete with the cast of the current game. You will have to face a series of bosses (six in total) from the old Tales of in order to finish this quest. You can find here our detailed guide on each of the bosses to defeat in order to complete the quest. So, after each boss defeated, you will get the infernal weapon of a character, with Alphen's weapon obtained last.

HOW DO THE INFERNAL WEAPONS WORK?

The first time you got these weapons, you might have thought they were very bad, especially considering the bosses you had to beat to get them. That's because they have a very special gimmick: With each enemy you defeat, their attack and elemental attack (the power always stays the same) increases by 1. Basically, the more enemies you kill with a character, the more powerful their infernal weapon becomes. With a maximum of 9999, this makes them potentially the most powerful weapons in the game. However, there are several details to take into account to understand what this means:

-It must be the character who kills the enemy, not someone else

-All enemies killed before obtaining the weapon are counted

-There is no need to have the weapon equipped for the kill to be counted

-The player does not have to kill the enemy for the kill to be counted, those made by the AI when you are not controlling the character also count

-The number of kills is automatically transferred to NG+, no artifact needed (but it also implies that it's impossible to prevent the transfer so you don't get overpowered at the beginning of your NG+)

FARMER LES KILLS

Now that you have your weapons and understand how they work, all you have to do is make them incredibly powerful. To do this, it's easy: just go to the Training Ground (Menancia - Viscint) and do the novice solo challenge for the character you want to farm kills for. Since you're probably already pretty far into the post-game, the challenge shouldn't take more than five seconds, and you can repeat it immediately unlike encounters with wild zeugles.

Team Member Guide

On this page of our complete Tales of Arise solution, you will find a guide dedicated to each character in the team. These guides are intended to explain how to exploit each character's unique strengths, their strengths and how to make the most of them, how to use their Artes, and in what situations you can use them.

Alphen

In keeping with the traditions of the series, each playable character in Tales of Arise has very distinct characteristics and the way to play each of them is therefore very different, as you have to take into account their strengths and weaknesses. Let's first take a look at how to play the main character of the game, Alphen.

Like all the main characters in the Tales of, Alphen is the easiest character to pick up and control, and you can get away with doing the whole adventure with him (although it would be a real shame to miss out on the strengths of the other team members).

The fact that this is a mainly melee character makes it easy to learn how to do basic combos. It is especially useful to learn the synergies between ground artes that send the character into the air, air artes that allow you to extend the combo into the air, and air artes that send the enemy back to the ground. For example, you can start with some basic attacks, Devouring Blade/Demonic Fang for a first arte, Flight of the wyvern to send the enemy in the air, again some basic attacks then Hurricane Strike to keep the enemy in the air, then Mirage/Falcon Flight to send the enemy back to the ground and repeat the operation.

If Alphen's basic artes are already very interesting, their "fiery" version, Alphen's strong point, is even more spectacular. After using an Arte (ground or air), you can hold the key to trigger the highlight and launch the "fiery" version of the arte. These are very generally much more powerful versions, with the elemental affinity Fire, and usually make enemies waver very quickly. Note that this version of the Arte will usually have the opposite (or neutral) role of the basic Arte, but rarely the same. For example, while Envol de la wyvern can send the enemy into the air, Envol du Phoenix sends them straight back to the ground

The major counterpart of Alphen's strong point is that to trigger the "fiery" version, it is necessary to sacrifice HP each time you use it. If this sacrifice is not to be neglected, it should not discourage you from using his strong point. Indeed, the more HP you sacrifice, the more damage you will inflict. With some skills activated, you will be able to sacrifice almost your entire life bar to be able to inflict simply enormous damage, and will melt the life bar of the bosses. You really shouldn't hesitate to sacrifice as much health as possible, even if it means being down to 1 health. After attacking, you can simply move back to take cover, and wait for an ally to heal you, or even use an item if you are really afraid of dying.

This is even more effective when you perform a fiery version of an Arte on a downed enemy. Alphen's Bonus Strike allows you to knock down any enemy without any conditions. So, as soon as your Bonus Strike is available, make sure you have full life, knock the enemy down, and sacrifice all your HP. If the damage would have been impressive in the first place, it will be even more so here since the enemy is down, making your hits even stronger.

Shionne

Shionne is simply the best healer of the group (there is not much competition, of course), with direct access to "First Aid", reanimation with "Resurrection" and healing for state alterations with "Recovery". However, when you control it, you should not hesitate to delegate the healer role to someone else (Dohalim for example, or use items) because playing the role of the team healer in a Tales of, it probably does not interest you

Fortunately, Shionne is also very interesting offensively. She can attack enemies from a distance without having to wait to cast a spell like with Rinwell and Dohalim (although she also has such artes). Her firearm allows her to be very effective against airborne enemies, and she easily knocks them down with her artes involving her rifle.

Generally speaking, Shionne's ground artes are very diverse: ranged attacks, spells, healing, but also explosive strikes, a type of attack that is exclusive to him. Shionne has indeed the possibility to throw grenades, often elemental, which allow you to complete your combos and inflict state alterations. If simply throwing the grenade allows you to launch a first attack, you can trigger a much more devastating attack by holding the key. There is often no point in not charging the grenade, so be sure to use the attack at the right time during your combo as this slight loading time must be taken into account.

Another factor to consider when using grenades is that Shionne has a stockpile of grenades, the number of which is listed at the top right of her life bar. When she runs out of grenades, Shionne can still use the primary version of artes with grenades, but she must first reload to use the higher version. To do this, you can either perform a basic attack when your supply is empty, in which case Shionne will reload before attacking, or reload at any time by pressing L2 and R1 at the same times

Last but not least, Shionne's strong point is that she is the best way to inflict state alterations on enemies, including bosses. Indeed, many skills in her titles allow her to increase the rate of alterations, and for reminder, these skills are cumulative. Also, most of his Elemental Artes have the side effect of inflicting alterations. With access to Fire, Water, Darkness, and Light Artes, Shionne can inflict poison, curse, freeze, and paralysis. Knowing that these alterations can be stacked on a single target, you can quickly render overpowered bosses completely harmless.

Rinwell

Rinwell is obviously the black mage of the team. She has a lot of elemental attacks, which makes her particularly useful for exploiting elemental weaknesses.

As far as ground spells are concerned, most of them are elemental spells that require a more or less important delay before they can be cast, depending on their power. For this kind of spell, it is generally advisable to move as far as possible from where the enemies are so as not to be threatened by the opponent's attacks when you take the time to cast a spell. Unlike the old Tales of however, you can move while a spell is loading (you have to unlock the corresponding skill), and above all you are not immediately interrupted when you are attacked, which makes it easier to get the hang of the character.

Unlike its ground artes, its air artes have no loading time and are more intended to complete a combo initiated by your allies or a ground arte. These artes also have an elemental affinity allowing you to continue to exploit weaknesses. The idea is to complement ground artes, which are generally massive and destructive attacks with air artes or other ground artes but are more intended to be used in close combat to create combos with Rinwell.

However, to be able to do very impressive combos with Rinwell, you have to use his strong point. Indeed, if you hold down the key when you cast a spell, you can delay the casting of the spell. Now, if you press R1 (basic attack key), Rinwell will store that same spell and charge it. What this means in practical terms is that when you go to use another spell, Rinwell will cast that spell first and then the stored spell, and that's what makes for really big combos and wobbling enemies.

Even better, this technique allows you to cast super-powered artes that you probably don't have access to yet. This is possible by casting the loaded version of the spell. To do this, either cast the same spell twice (if you store Air Shock, then use Air Shock again, you'll cast Cross Blade), or store a spell of one item, then cast another higher-ranked arte of the same rank. For example, if you store Air Shock and then use Cross Blade, you will cast Cyclone. This last method is probably the easiest way to cast destructive spells with Rinwell, since you can store a beginner's arte very quickly and it doesn't take long to load, and then cast an intermediate arte to activate an overpowered arte.

Note that this technique is also possible for Rinwell's support skills. For example, if you first store Acuity, then use Acuity again, you will launch the buff on the whole team. Be careful though, don't forget that support skills also consume SP, and these buffs are very greedy so you shouldn't abuse them too much, at least at the beginning of the game when your SP gauge is limited.

One of the big advantages of Rinwell is that his most powerful spells are very massive attacks that cover almost the entire arena, which has the following benefits:

-They are very difficult to avoid, very useful against very mobile enemies

-They allow to eliminate the mobs accompanying the bosses very quickly

-They allow you to hit the weak points (orange core) of the bosses without any risk since you attack from a distance. If the enemy has several of them, you will hit them all, which is even better.

If you don't like playing as a mage, but still want to keep Rinwell on the team, consider setting the "Stay away from enemies" action in your strategy, with "Always" and "No restrictions" so that she stays as far away from enemies as possible when she casts her spells (be careful, a strategy applies to all your allies, so be sure it doesn't interfere with the behavior of your other characters)

Law

Like Alphen, Law is a primarily hand-to-hand character, with a few supporting artes to either maintain his life or his offense. Because Law's moves are so fast and powerful, he can easily wobble enemies and get bonus hits quickly, especially if he exploits elemental weaknesses. This makes him a very simple character to learn how to do long and powerful melee combos.

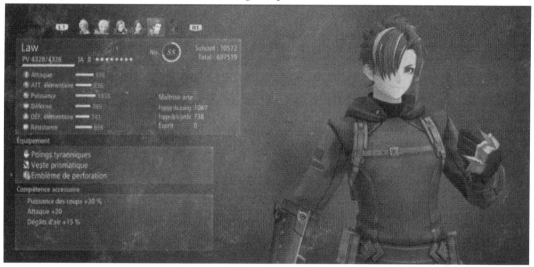

Thanks to his strong point, his physical and elemental attacks become even more powerful, and he can even more easily make enemies stagger and get bonus hits. To trigger his strong point, all you have to do is link a certain number of attacks without being hit. A blue, then yellow flame appears around his hands and feet to indicate that the sweet spot is active, with the yellow light providing an even more powerful boost than the blue light.

This power point remains active as long as Law is not hit, but it can stop if a certain amount of time passes without you managing to hit the enemy (sometimes, even if you get hit, the aura does not disappear). In fact, it is necessary to be very aggressive when you control Law, but it is also necessary to be careful not to get hit so as not to lose the bonus. Taking damage is often very bad with Law because, in addition to losing the bonus, Law has very bad defenses, so it is not uncommon to see him die very quickly, especially if you leave him to the AI.

Law's elemental covariance is very interesting, and makes Law probably the most versatile character on the team since he can cover all weaknesses except for Darkness. With his Steel Arte buffing his attack and elemental attack by 30%, Law is clearly one of the best at exploiting elemental weaknesses among physical characters.

In short, if all you want to do is hit monsters the old fashioned way with your hands and feet, with simple combos that do a lot of damage, Law is clearly your character. Be careful not to fall into the trap of being too gruff though, because if you can't dodge, Law won't last long in battle.

Another problem with Law is that if you don't control him yourself, the AI is not good enough to dodge attacks regularly. This has several negative consequences: - On the one hand, Law will rarely be able to use his strength and have attack boosts since the AI will regularly lose him - Due to his low defense and HP, he will be knocked out quite often, especially in the higher difficulties.

Kisara

If you like counter and parry mechanics, this character is for you. Kisara is basically the tank of the team, with average offensive skills, but which can be improved with well executed parries, and with incomparable defenses. Her main gimmick is the fact that, unlike all the other team members, Kisara does not dodge but uses her shield to parry and defend.

In fact, it excels against all enemies that have one or more charge attacks, and there is really no reason not to include it in the team (or even play it) when facing this kind of enemy. Indeed, if you defend when an enemy is about to charge you, you will perform a perfect defense, which will directly knock the enemy down. A yellow light also appears around the shield to indicate that your arrows now do more damage and are harder to block.

Some artes like Lion's Roar also become even more powerful if you perform them with the guard up. These artes should be used to counter enemies and initiate your combos, so you can follow up with more traditional artes.

Surprisingly, Kisara also has a few support and healing spells (Protective Aura for example), which can deal damage while healing/helping your team. These spells should be seen more as a way to counter enemies than a way to heal yourself, Kisara will never properly replace Shionne and Dohalim for healing.

Dohalim

Dohalim is more or less a jack of all trades: he has melee, healing, spells, and support skills. A character with such diversity has several advantages.

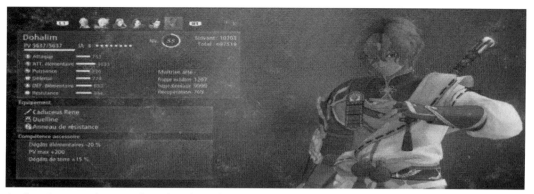

At first, he can take over the role of another character while the latter does something else. For example, if the boss you're fighting is a bird, you'd better use Shionne offensively, and Dohalim can take care of him. Similarly, he can come and help another character in his role (assist Alphen and/or Law in close combat, or Rinwell by casting spells for example).

Dohalim is also interesting because of his strong point. Whenever you make a perfect dodge, his staff extends in the same way as Leia in Tales of Xillia. When his staff is extended, not only does he have a longer range, but his attacks will more easily interrupt enemies, and his critical rate increases. The beneficial effects of the elongated staff can be greatly enhanced by the many skills available with its different titles (more damage, increased critical hit rate, longer duration...).

To perform combos with Dohalim, you can start with a spell that requires a loading time, which will probably make the enemy wobble, before moving on to physical artes. Like Law, being able to dodge attacks is necessary to get the most out of his abilities.

As a mage, Dohalim is very efficient. He is also the only one, with Shionne, to have access to Dark Arts. Thus, a very interesting strategy to implement if you don't want to play Dohalim directly is to form a team with three mages: one white mage (Shionne) and two black mages (Rinwell and Dohalim). Add an action "Stay away from enemies" with the conditions "Always" and "no restriction" to make sure that all three stay away from enemies to cast their spell. You, meanwhile, play a physical character that serves as a decoy for the enemies. This way, your mages can quietly bombard the enemies while they desperately try to hit you.

The titles

On this page of our complete Tales of Arise solution, you will find the complete list of titles for each character, how to unlock them, and what skills you can get in exchange for your Skill Points (SP) earned by doing battles and side quests.

List of Alphen's qualifications and skills

Titles are back in Tales of Arise. They have a capital importance since they directly impact the statistical progression of your characters and give them many important bonuses. Here are the 15 titles obtainable with Alphen, their skills and how to unlock them

IRON MASK

-Increased JA max capacity

-Increased critical damage

-Improved perfect dodge/guard

-Increased air damage

-Sonic Strike (Arte)

Completion Bonus: Attack +10

How to get it : The title is automatically obtained during the prologue in the Kingdom of Calaglia

THE ARDENT SWORD

-Torrent infernal (Arte)

-Extension of Fiery Edge

-Increased damage on the ground

-Faster Fiery Slash charge

-Flight of the Phoenix (Arte)

Completion Bonus: Defense +10

How to get it : The title is automatically obtained during the prologue in the Kingdom of Calaglia

NOTHING NEW UNDER THE SUN

-Counterattack after defeating an enemy

-Increased bonus strike damage

-Increased counterattack damage

-JA restoration after perfect dodge/guard

-Flight of the Falcon (Arte)

Completion Bonus : Elemental Attack +30

How to get it: The title is obtained after spending time with a companion for the first time at a campfire.

A COMMON IDEAL: FREEDOM

-Increased JA max capacity

-Extended Hos-limits

-Air jump

-Increased damage in counter-attack

-Tearing Wave (Arte)

Completion Bonus : Elemental Attack +40

How to get it : The title is automatically obtained during the main adventure in the kingdom of Menancia.

ETERNAL FIRE

-Increased JA max capacity

-Faster Fiery Slice charge

-Increased dodge distance

-Extended Fiery Slice

-Burning Wave (Arte)

Completion Bonus : Resistance +50

How to obtain : The title is obtained automatically after defeating Efrit Malum

REBEL SPARKLE

-Counter-attack

-Star Dust (Arte)

-JA max capacity increase

-Aerial dodge

-Cutting Wind (Arte)

Completion Bonus : Defense +10

How to obtain : The title is obtained automatically during the prologue in the Kingdom of Calaglia

RELEASE EMISSARY

Faster JA recovery

JA restoration after perfect dodge/guard

Increased weak point damage

Increased defense/near-death elemental defense

Increased JA max capacity

Completion Bonus: Elemental Defense +20

How to get it : The title is automatically obtained during the prologue in the Kingdom of Calaglia

ARDENT SHOT

-Bonus gauge increase after enemy down

-Extension of Burning Edge

-JA restoration after critical hits

-Increased defense/defense elemental imminent death

-Tearing Lightning(Arte)

Completion Bonus : Resistance +20

How to get it : The title is obtained after having performed 35 bonus attacks

THE POWER OF THE RULER

-Increased bonus strike damage

-Easier off limits

-Extended Fiery Edge

-Increased attack/elemental attack imminent death

-Blade of Nothingness (Arte)

Completion Bonus: Attack +50

How to get it : The title is obtained after defeating the fifth lord during the main story.

UNDEFEATED SWORDSMAN

-Increased normal attack limit

-Easier off-limits

-Faster JA recovery

-Increased air damage

-Void Lightning (Arte)

Completion Bonus: Power +30

How to get it : The title is obtained after completing the solo novice challenge """ with Alphen at the Training Ground in Viscint.

WEAPON COLLECTOR

-Increased JA max capacity

-Increased critical damage

-JA restoration after critical hits

-Increased near death elemental attack/attack

-Devastation (Arte)

Completion Bonus : Elemental Defense +30

How to get it : The title is obtained after having forged 10 different weapons

ARMOLOGIST

-Increase of the limit of normal attacks

-Increased critical damage

-Perfect dodge/guard made easier

-Increased weak point damage

-Faster JA recovery

Completion Bonus: Power +40

How to get it : The title is obtained after forging the weapon "Blade of atonement".

PAPILLAE OF HELL

-Recover before you are down

-Increased critical hit rate on counter-attack

-Knockout repelled

-Increased attack/elemental attack imminent death

-Iron Cutter (Arte)

Completion Bonus : Attack +20

How to get it : The title is obtained after cooking roasted chicken with Alphen

WINNER OF THE FOUR LIGHTS

-Increase JA max capacity

-Increased damage on the ground

-Increased critical hit rate on counterattack

-Increased bonus gauge after enemy down

-Thunder Devastation (Arte)

Completion Bonus : Elemental Attack +50

How to get it : The title can be obtained after completing the following side quests:

-Nevira's Spectral Flower

-Spiritual Temple

-Farewell, dear mage

-A mad rage

ENRICHING LINK

-JA max capacity increase

-Extended Out of Bounds

-K.O. postponed

-Increased damage bonus strike

-Lightning Fang (Arte)

Completion Bonus : Elemental Defense +40

How to get it : The title is obtained after maximizing the bond of affection with a team member.

VETERAN SAMURAI (DLC)

-Increased attack/elemental attack after eating

-Increased attack/elemental attack if multiple enemies

-Knockout repelled

-Increased attack/elemental attack on impending death

-Orochi's Fury (Arte)

Completion Bonus : Attack +50

How to get it : DLC

BEACH HERO (DLC)

-Reinforced counterattack

-Increased bonus damage after alteration

-Increased bonus damage after alteration

-Enhanced counterattack

-Howling Azure Storm (Arte)

Completion Bonus : Elemental Attack +50

How to get it : DLC

STILTED STUDENT (DLC)

-Increased bonus gauge after victory

-Fill bonus gauge every 10 moves

-Increased bonus gauge gain after victory

-JB refill at the beginning of the fight

-Plasma shock (Arte)

Completion bonus : Elemental attack +50

How to get it : DLC

List of Shionne's qualifications

Titles are back in Tales of Arise. They have a capital importance since they directly impact the statistical progression of your characters and give them many important bonuses. Here are the 15 titles obtainable with Shionne, their skills and how to unlock them.

QUEEN OF ESCAPE

-JA max capacity increase

-Volcanic Strike (Arte)

-KO repelled

-Increased Attack/Elemental Attack imminent death

-Aquatic Gemini (Arte)

Completion Bonus : Elemental Defense +10

How to obtain : The title is obtained automatically during the main story in the kingdom of Calaglia

A SPICY WOMAN

-Ignis Celestra (Arte)

-Increased air damage

-Increased resistance while launching an Arte

-Increased JA max capacity

-Lunar Explosion (Arte)

Completion Bonus : Resistance +10

How to get it : The title is obtained automatically during the main story in the kingdom of Calaglia

HEALER

-Improved healing skills

-Increased bonus gauge after enemy down

-Expanded off-limits

-Faster JA recovery

-Healing Circles (Arte)

Completion Bonus: Elemental Attack +30

How to get it : The title can be obtained after completing the side quest A Healer and Her Patients (Menancia - Observation Center)

CRAZY TRIGGER-HAPPY

-Increase JA max capacity

-Mobility launch Arte

-Easier off-limits

-Increase in the rate of alterations

-Lunar Corruption (Arte)

Completion bonus : Attack +30

How to obtain : The title is obtained automatically during the main story in the kingdom of Menancia

GODDESS OF KINDNESS

-Increase JA capacity max

-Restore JA after victory

-Improvement of the healing artes

-Reduced arte casting time during a combo

-Aqueous Impact (Arte)

Completion Bonus : Elemental Defense +40

How to get it : The title is obtained after healing 10 NPCs

INSTANT KITCHEN

-Counterattack

-Increase in the rate of alterations

-Increased Attack/Elemental Death Attack

-Increased bonus damage after alterations

-Toxicity (Arte)

Completion bonus : Attack +10

How to obtain : The title is obtained after cooking 1 meal.

AN INSATIABLE APPETITE

-Increased Attack/Elemental Attack after eating

-Faster JA recovery

-Restore SP after eating

-Increased normal attack limit

-Spear Sweep (Arte)

Completion Bonus: Resistance +30

How to get it : The title is obtained after cooking 8 meals.

GREATER CLASS

-Increased JA max capacity

-Faster JA recovery

-Refill JB at the beginning of the fight

-Increased bonus gauge after enemy down

-Geyser (Arte)

Completion bonus : Defense +20

How to get it : The title is obtained after having made 4 accessories.

FASHIONISTA

-Increase of the limit of normal attacks

-Filling JB at the beginning of the fight

-Increased damage on weak point

-Perfect dodge/guard made easier

-Dissipation (Arte)

Completion bonus : Resistance +50

How to get it : The title is obtained after forging the "Mystic Emblem" accessory which is unlocked by completing Shionne's advanced solo challenge at the Training Ground (Menancia - Viscint).

THE LAST LADY

-Increase JA max capacity

-Increased resistance while launching an Arte

-Reduced arte casting time during a combo

-Restore SP after eating

-Revitalization (Arte)

Completion bonus : Elemental attack +40

How to get it : The title is obtained during the main story, in the forbidden zone.

A REAL BOMB

-Recovery before you hit the ground

-Increased special ammunition capacity

-Last shot

-Increased bonus hit damage

-Glacio Celestra (Arte)

Completion bonus : Power +20

How to get it : The title is obtained after exploding 50 grenades in combat with Shionne.

SNIPER

-Counterattack after victory

-Increased air damage

-Air dodge

-Bonus gauge increase after enemy down

-JA restoration after victory

Completion Bonus : Power +20

How to get it : The title is obtained after knocking down 20 airborne enemies with Shionne's Bonus Strike.

INSECT SLAYER

-Increased JA max capacity

-Extended off-limits

-Increased bonus damage after alterations

-Easier off-limits

-Increased air damage

Completion Bonus: Defense +40

How to get it : The title is obtained after completing the side quest "A place for her" (Ganath Haros - Shining Waterfall Wood).

CHIEF OF THE HEART

-Improved healing arts

-Increased bonus damage after alterations

-Increased Elemental Attack after eating

-Increased weak point damage

-Increased bonus strike damage

Completion Bonus : Elemental Defense +50

How to get it: The title is obtained after discovering the recipe for Shionne's Pancakes. After obtaining it, go camping to trigger a scene and obtain the title.

ELITE ARTIFICER

-Increased JA max capacity

-Increased special ammo capacity

-Increase of the rate of alterations

--Last shot

Explosion (Arte)

Completion Bonus : Power +50

How to get it : The title can be obtained after completing the side quest "Cloud of Hell" (Mahag Saar - Secret Port).

SCARLET WARRIOR (DLC)

--Instant Cyan (Arte)

Restore HP after eating

-Restore HP after eating

-Increased Elemental Attack after eating

-Increased Attack/Elemental Attack after eating

Completion Bonus : Elemental Attack +50

How to get it : DLC

QUEEN OF THE SEAS (DLC)

-Ice tornado (Arte)

-Increase of the rate of alterations

-Increased bonus damage after damage

-Increased bonus damage after damage

-Increased damage rate

Completion Bonus : Power +50

How to get it : DLC

THE NEWS (DLC)

-Ray (Arte)

-Increased bonus gauge gain after victory

-Fill up bonus gauge every 10 moves

-Fill bonus gauge every 10 moves

-Increase bonus gauge gain after victory

Completion Bonus : Elemental Defense +50

How to get it : DLC

List of Rinwell's qualifications and skills

Titles are back in Tales of Arise. They have a capital importance since they directly impact the statistical progression of your characters and give them many important bonuses. Here are the 15 titles obtainable with Rinwell, their skills and how to unlock them

MAGE DAHNIENNE

-Increased JA max capacity

-Enhanced magical charge

-JA restoration after critical hits

-Increased damage on weak point

-Thunder Blade (Arte)

Completion bonus: Elemental defense +10

How to obtain : Basic title

SILVER SWORD

-Increase of JA max capacity

-Puddle of water (Arte)

-Mobility launch Arte

-Reduction of Arte launch time during a combo

-Burst (Arte)

Completion bonus : Defense +10

How to obtain : The title is obtained automatically during the main story in the kingdom of Cyslodia

RETIRED AVENGER

-Increase JA max capacity

-Increased damage on the ground

-Increased dodge distance

-Reduced arte casting time during a combo

-Holy Lance (Arte)

Completion bonus: Resistance +30

How to get it : The title is obtained automatically during the main story in the kingdom of Ganath Haros

A FINE PERCEPTION

-Increased normal attack limit

-Increased bonus hit damage

-Extended off-limits

-Enhanced magic charge

-Crossed Blade (Arte)

Completion Bonus: Power +40

How to get it : The title is obtained automatically during the main story in Anchor

PRINCESS OF LIGHTNING

-Increase JA capacity max

-JA restoration after critical hits

-Increased ground damage

-Increased anti-dragon damage

-Divine Sword (Arte)

Completion Bonus : Elemental Attack +50

How to get it: The title is obtained after completing the side quest "Mistress of Nature" (Ganath Haros - Pelegion - 2nd Level).

FRIEND OF THE BIRDS

-Increase JA capacity max

-JA restoration after victory

-Increased bonus gauge gain after victory

-Astral energy owls

-Concentration (Arte)

Completion bonus : Resistance +10

How to get it : The title is obtained after having launched the side quest "The owl forest" (automatically obtained during the main story in Cyslodia)

FEATHER FAN

-Astral energy owls

-Increased damage on weak point

-Increased bonus gauge gain after victory

-JB refill at the beginning of the fight

-Increased bonus gauge after enemy down

Completion bonus : Resistance +40

How to get it : The title is obtained after finding 31 owls and talking to the owl king.

SPELL NEUTRALIZER

-Flight of the Swallow (Arte)

-Filling JB at the beginning of the fight

-Increased bonus gauge after victory

-Air jump

-Increase in bonus gauge after enemy down

Completion bonus : Elemental defense +20

How to get it : The title is obtained after stopping 6 spells with Rinwell's Bonus Strike

INVINCIBLE MAGE

-Increased resistance while casting an arte

-Increased air damage

-JA restoration after victory

-Air dodge

-Increased JA max capacity

Completion Bonus: Elemental Attack +20

How to get it: The title is obtained after completing the solo novice challenge with Rinwell at the Training Ground (Menancia - Viscint).

TUMULTUOUS MAGE

-Increased resistance while casting an Arte

-Enhanced magic charge

-Counterattack after victory

-Extended off-limits

-Tidal wave (Arte)

Completion bonus : Elemental defense +50

How to obtain : The title is obtained after completing the side quest "A mad rage" (Ganath Haros - Thistlym)

ETERNAL STUDENT

-Counterattack

-Recover before you are down

-Faster magic charge

-Increased bonus gauge after enemy down

-Acuity (Arte)

Completion bonus: Elemental attack +20

How to get it : The title is obtained after finding 15% of the items (75/500)

DOCTOR OF ITEM HISTORY

-Increase JA max capacity

-Increased air damage

-Faster magic charge

-Increased resistance while casting an Arte

-Faster JA recovery

Completion bonus: Power +40

How to obtain : The title is obtained after finding 50% of the items (250/500)

BIBLIOPHILE

-Increased JA max capacity

-Celestial Hammer (Arte)

-Increased anti-dragon damage

-Faster JA recovery

-Ice Thrower (Arte)

Completion bonus: Elemental attack +30

How to get it : The title is obtained after completing the side quest "The Bibliophile" (Menancia - Autelina Palace - Library)

SWEET BECAUSE

-Rise of the waters (Arte)

-Increased damage on land

-JA restoration after critical hits

-KO repelled

-JA restoration after victory

Completion bonus: Power +30

How to get it: The title is obtained after cooking ice cream with Rinwell for the first time.

AIR CURRENT

-Faster JA recovery

-Increased bonus hit damage

-Increased weak point damage

-JB refill at the beginning of the fight

-Cyclone (Arte)

Completion bonus : Power +50

How to obtain : The title is obtained after completing the side quest "Tornadoes by the Sea" (Ganath Haros - Thistlym).

DEMON DARK RAVEN (DLC)

-Wind Fang (Arte)

-Increased damage on the ground

-Increased weak point damage

-Increased air damage

-Increased ground damage

Completion Bonus: Elemental Attack +50

How to get it : DLC

AUSTERE SWIMMER (DLC)

-Burst of arrows (Arte)

-Increased critical damage

-KO repelled

-Increased critical damage

-Reduced arte casting time during a combo

Completion Bonus: Elemental Defense +50

How to get it : DLC

PLAYFUL STUDENT (DLC)

-Divine Ray (Arte)

-Fill bonus gauge every 10 moves

-Fill bonus gauge every 10 moves

-Filling bonus gauge every 10 moves

-Reduction of arte launch time during a combo

Completion bonus : Power +50

How to get it : DLC

List of Law's credentials

Titles are back in Tales of Arise. They have a capital importance since they directly impact the statistical progression of your characters and give them many important bonuses. Here are the 15 titles obtainable with Law, their skills and how to unlock them

WIRE ROPE

-Increased JA max capacity

-Increased awakening attack power

-Increased dodge distance

-Increased counterattack damage

-Tectonic Punch (Arte)

Completion bonus: Attack +10

How to obtain : Basic title

RENÉGAT

-Counterattack

-JA regeneration after victory

-Awakening extension

-JA restoration after critical hits

-Eagle Plunge (Arte)

Completion bonus : Power +10

How to obtain : Basic title

THE REBIRTH OF THE SILVER WOLF

-Air jump

-JA restoration after perfect dodge/guard

-JA restoration after critical hits

-JB refill at the beginning of a fight

-Lightning tornado (Arte)

Completion bonus : Elemental attack +20

How to get it : The title is automatically unlocked during the main story in the kingdom of Menancia

MEDIATOR

-Increased JA max capacity

-KO repelled

-Increased Attack/Elemental Attack near death

-Increased attack power while awake

-Inspiration (Arte)

Completion bonus : Resistance +30

How to get it : The title unlocks automatically during the main story in the kingdom of Mahag Saar

EXCEPTIONAL FIGHTER, EXCEPTIONALLY LEFT

-Increased JA max capacity

-Reinforced counter-attack

-Bonus to chain fights while awake

-Increased critical damage

-Inferno punch (Arte)

Completion bonus: Elemental attack +40

How to get it : The title is automatically unlocked during the main story in the kingdom of Ganath Haros

PRINCE OF IRON FISTS

-Off-limits facility in awakening

-JB refill at the beginning of a fight

-JA restoration after victory

-Refill bonus gauge every 10 moves

-Dragon Throw (Arte)

Completion bonus : Attack +20

How to get it : The title is unlocked after 3 bonus hits with Law

ARMOR BREAKER

-JA restoration after perfect dodge/guard

-Reduction of awakening conditions

-Out of bounds ease in awakening

-Increased bonus hit damage

-Increased bonus gauge after enemy down

Completion bonus: Power +40

How to get it: The title is unlocked after breaking the armor of 40 enemies with Law's Bonus Strike.

THE NOODLE

-Counterattack after victory

-Bonus gauge increase after enemy down

-Air dodge

-Faster JA recovery

-Bonus for chaining fights while awake

Completion bonus: Defense +10

How to get it : The title is unlocked after completing the side quest "Pharia's Ranch" (Menancia - Traslida Road)

THE FRIEND OF THE BEASTS

-Bonus for fighting while awake

-JA restoration after victory

-Increased Defense/Elemental Defense near death

-Filling JB at the beginning of the fight

-JA restoration after perfect dodge/guard

Completion bonus: Defense +50

How to get it : The title is unlocked after having raised the six animals available at the ranch.

CALVES OF STEEL

-Increased JA max capacity

-Increased attack power when awake

-Enhanced counterattack

-Easier off-limits while awake

-Super Swallow Dance (Arte)

Completion bonus : Resistance +40

How to get it: The title unlocks after reaching 700 in Arte Leg Strike Mastery.

INDESTRUCTIBLE FISTS

-Increased normal attack limit

-Increased max JA capacity

-Faster JA recovery

-Bonus gauge refill every 10 hits

-Easier off-limits

Completion bonus: Attack +30

How to get it : The title is unlocked after completing the Novice Solo Challenge with Law at the Training Ground (Menancia - Viscint).

BOUNTY HUNTER

-Increased JA max capacity

-Increased bonus gauge after enemy down

-Enhanced counterattack

-Facilitated off-limits

-Reduction of the conditions of awakening

Completion bonus : Elemental defense +30

How to get it : The title is unlocked after completing the side quest "Bounty Hunt" (Menancia - Viscint)

IN FULL GROWTH

-Recover before you go down

-Increased counterattack damage

-Increased Attack/Elemental Death Attack

-Increased bonus strike damage

-Bolero of Fangs (Arte)

Completion Bonus: Elemental Defense +20

How to obtain : The title is unlocked after cooking 7 dishes with Law

SPACE CHAMPION

-Increased JA max capacity

-Increased critical damage

-JA restoration after critical hits

-Easier off-limits

-Illuminated Mirage (Arte)

Completion bonus : Elemental attack +50

How to get it : The title unlocks after completing the side quest "An ambition fulfilled" (Other - Daeq Faezol - Lower Level)

FLAG HOLDER

-Increased normal attack limit

-Fills bonus gauge every 10 hits

-Increased critical damage

-Faster JA recovery

-Increased awakening time

Completion bonus : Attack +50

How to get it : The title is unlocked after completing the side quest « Conflicting Feelings » (Calaglia – Ulzebek)

CLUMSY NINJA (DLC)

-Dark Wind (Arte)

-Extended off-limits

-Easy off-limits for the group

-Out of bounds easy for the group

-Extended off-limits

Completion bonus : Attack +50

How to get it : DLC

APPLIED DIVER (DLC)

-Snake Fist (Arte)

-Increased air damage

-KO repelled

-Increased ground damage

-Improved perfect dodge/guard

Completion bonus: Power +50

How to get it : DLC

FANFARON (DLC)

-Sparkling wild roar (Arte)

-Increased damage on weak point

-Increased bonus gauge gain after victory

-Increased bonus gauge gain after victory

-Increased weak point damage

Completion Bonus: Attack +50

How to get it : DLC

List of Kisara's titles and skills

Titles are back in Tales of Arise. They have a capital importance since they directly impact the statistical progression of your characters and give them many important bonuses. Here are the 15 titles obtainable with Kisara, their skills and how to unlock them.

CAPTAIN KISARA

-Increased JA max capacity

-Easier off-limits

-Increased guard effects

-Guard mobility

-Increased gauge gain after victory

Completion bonus : Attack +10

How to obtain : Basic title

DEVOTED SISTER

-Counter-attack

-Increased JA max capacity

-Recovery before going down

-Increased Defense/Elemental Death Defense

-Counterattack after victory

Completion bonus : Power +10

How to obtain : Basic title

IDEALIST

-Increase JA capacity max

-Increased Elemental Attack/Attack if multiple enemies

-Increase of the effects of the guard

-Increased Elemental Attack/Attack after guard

-Crossfire (Arte)

Completion bonus : Elemental attack +40

How to get it : The title is automatically unlocked during the main story after defeating the fifth lord

BENEVOLENT SHIELD

-Enhanced aggression during guarding

-Easy off-limits for the group

-JB refill at the beginning of the fight

-Increased Elemental Attack/Attack if multiple enemies

-Slag attack (Arte)

Completion bonus : Defense +50

How to get it : The title is automatically unlocked during the main story in the kingdom of Menancia

INDOMITABLE GOLDEN LIONESS

-Increased JA max capacity

-Reinforced warnings

-Filling JB at the beginning of the fight

-Increased guard effects

-Spear of Light (Arte)

Completion bonus : Resistance +50

How to get it : The title unlocks after completing the advanced solo challenge with Kisara at the Training Ground (Menancia - Viscint).

INDESTRUCTIBLE WALL

-Faster JA recovery

-Increased bonus gauge after enemy down

-JB refill at the beginning of the fight

-Increased bonus gauge after victory

-Crescent moon (Arte)

Completion bonus : Defense +10

How to get it : The title is unlocked after blocking an enemy's charge with Kisara's bonus strike

FLAWLESS FIGHTER

-Increased counterattack damage

-Increased critical hit rate on counterattack

-Filling JA after victory

-Increased aggression while on guard

-Series of lightning bolts (Arte)

Completion bonus : Resistance +20

How to get it : The title unlocks after completing the solo novice challenge with Kisara at the Training Ground (Menancia - Viscint)

SPRAY SHIELD

-Increased Elemental Attack/Attack after Guard

-Reinforced guards

-Easier off-limits for the group

-Increased counterattack damage

-Lion's Roar (Arte)

Completion bonus: Elemental defense +30

How to get it : The title is unlocked after completing the side quest "Walking Rock" (Menancia - Viscint)

MIGALPEDIA

-Off-limits made easy

-Avenging Guard

-Increased bonus gauge gain after victory

-Increased bonus hit damage

-Assault of the Beast (Arte)

Completion bonus : Attack +20

How to get it : The title is unlocked after completing the side quest "Once a rival, always a rival" (Menancia - Viscint - Training ground)

HAMMER-ATOMIZER

-Increased JA max capacity

-Perfect dodge/guard made easier

-Increased bonus gauge after enemy down

-JA restoration after critical hits

-Maximum explosion (Arte)

Completion bonus : Attack +50

How to get it : The title is unlocked after obtaining 600 Arte Mastery in Powerful Strike.

SEASONED FISHERWOMAN

-Faster JA restoration

-Easier out of bounds

-Knockout repelled

-Air dodge

-Glowing Emission (Arte)

Completion bonus : Elemental defense +20

How to obtain : The title is unlocked after learning to fish.

QUEEN OF FISHING

-Increased JA max capacity

-Faster JA recovery

-Increased Defense/Elemental Defense near death

-JA restoration after critical hits

-Storm of Wyvern (Arte)

Completion bonus : Elemental attack +20

How to get it : The title is unlocked after catching 1 legendary fish (fish with two life bars)

STRONG AS A COW FISHERWOMAN

-Increased critical hit rate in counter-attack

-Increased JA max capacity

-Increased Attack/Elemental Death Attack

-Increased bonus strike damage

-Increased bonus gauge after enemy down

Completion bonus: Elemental attack +40

How to get it : The title is unlocked after catching the Silver Marlin

WHO WANTS FISH GETS WET!

-Increased normal attack limit

-Enhanced counterattack

-Increased critical hit rate on counterattack

-Increased counterattack damage

-Chaos Stab (Arte)

Completion bonus: Resistance +30

How to get it : The title is unlocked after cooking Sashimi for the first time.

CHEFFE EN CHEF

-Increased normal attack limit

-JA restoration after victory

-Reinforced warnings

-Enhanced counterattack

-Increased Elemental Attack/Attack after Guard

Completion Bonus : Power +40

How to get it : The title is unlocked after cooking 5 of Kisara's favorite dishes with her.

DEDICATED WARRIOR (DLC)

-Descending Storm (Arte)

-Increased air damage

-Faster JA recovery

-Increased ground damage

-Increased weak point damage

Completion bonus: Defense +50

How to get it : DLC

RELAXED LADY (DLC)

-Water Snake Groove (Arte)

-JA restoration after perfect dodge/guard

-Increased Elemental Attack/Immediate Death Attack

-Increased Attack/Elemental Attack imminent death

-JA restoration after perfect dodge/guard

Completion bonus : Elemental attack +50

How to get it : DLC

PASSIONATE HOME TEACHER (DLC)

=Dazzling Spin (Arte)

-Critical damage increase

-Increased Elemental Attack if multiple enemies

-Enhanced counterattack

-Increased critical damage

Completion Bonus: Attack +50

How to get it : DLC

List of Dohalim's titles and skills

Titles are back in Tales of Arise. They have a capital importance since they directly impact the statistical progression of your characters and give them many important bonuses. Here are the 15 titles obtainable with Dohalim, their skills and how to unlock them.

ARCHITECT OF COEXISTENCE

-JA max capacity increase

-Lionheart (Arte)

-Faster JA recovery

-Perfect dodge/guard made easier

-Catapult (Arte)

Completion bonus: Elemental defense +10

How to obtain : Basic title

EX-SEIGNOR

-Counter-attack

-Resurrection (Arte)

-Increased strike damage bonus

-Perfect dodge/guard made easier

-Negative Portal (Arte)

Completion bonus: Defense +10

How to obtain : Basic title

DILETTANTE

-Increased critical hits with Stick Extension

-Recovery before going down

-Increased damage on the ground

-Increased critical damage with Staff Extension

-Gravisphere (Arte)

Completion Bonus: Resistance +10

How to obtain : Basic title

RENIAN LEADER

-Increase JA max capacity

-Increased damage on the ground

-Improved healing artes

-Improved perfect dodge/guard

-Land Elk (Arte)

Completion bonus: Defense +50

How to get it : The title is automatically unlocked during the main story in Lenegis

EXCEPTIONAL MATCHMAKER

-Increased resistance while launching an arte

-Increased bonus strike damage

-Enhanced counterattack

-Increased critical damage

-Blood Flowers (Arte)

Completion Bonus : Resistance +50

How to get it : The title is unlocked after completing the side quest "The Missing Fiancé" (Ganath Haros - Thistlym)

UNDEFEATED LORD

-Max JA ability increase

-Air dodge

-Counterattack after victory

-Air jump

-Penumbra (Arte)

Completion bonus : Attack +20

How to get it : The title is unlocked after completing the solo novice challenge with Dohalim at the Training Ground (Menancia - Viscint).

MASTER OF PLANTS

-Increased JA max capacity

-Increased resistance while launching an arte

-Increased bonus gauge after enemy down

-JA restoration after perfect dodge/guard

-Solar captivity (Arte)

Completion bonus : Elemental attack +20

How to get it : The title is unlocked after 10 successful bonus strikes with Dohalim on fast enemies.

BLACK WITCH

-Increase JA max capacity

-Refill bonus gauge every 10 moves

-Reduced arte casting time during a combo

-Increased critical damage with Staff Extension

-Demon Spear (Arte)

Completion bonus: Elemental attack +40

How to get it: The title unlocks after obtaining 600 Arte Mastery in Demonic Strike.

TREASURE HUNTER

-Faster JA recovery

-Increased duration of Staff Extension

-JA restoration after perfect dodge/guard

-Amplified attack with Staff Extension

-Increased normal attack limit

Completion Bonus: Elemental Defense +20

How to get it: The title unlocks after finding your first artifact in the main story.

ANTIQUE COLLECTOR

-Increased critical damage

-JA restoration after critical hits

-Increased stick extension duration

-Increased bonus gauge after enemy down

-Amplified attack with Staff Extension

Completion Bonus: Elemental Defense +40

How to get it : The title is unlocked after finding 8 artifacts.

ETERNAL PROTECTOR

-Staff Extension Amplification

-Reduction of arte launch time during a combo

-Refill bonus gauge every 10 hits

-JA restoration after critical hits

-Regeneration (Arte)

Completion bonus: Power +40

How to get it : The title is unlocked after completing the side quest "Dohalim, the big game hunter".

LORD AND PATRON SAINT

-Increase JA capacity max

-Mobility launch arte

-Increased critical hits with stick extension

-Filling bonus gauge every 10 hits

-Increased bonus gauge after enemy down

Completion bonus : Attack+60

How to get it : The title is unlocked after completing the side quest "The owl sanctuary" (Mahag Saar - Niez)

POOR MATCHMAKER

-Increase of the limit of normal attacks

-Healing (Arte)

-Increased duration of Staff Extension

-Reinforced counter-attack

-Sonic Lance (Arte)

Completion bonus : Resistance +30

How to get it : The title is unlocked after completing the side quest "Their Future" (Ganath Haros - Pelegion level 3)

RARE COMMODITY EXPERT

-Staff Extension Amplification

-Healing Artes Enhancement

-JA restoration after critical hits

-Amplified attack with Staff Expansion

-Increased JA max capacity

Completion bonus: Power +30

How to get it: The title unlocks after cooking grilled Laporc with Dohalim for the first time.

DRINKING COMPANION

-KO repelled

-Increased critical strike with Staff Extension

-Increased critical damage with Staff Extension

-Faster JA recovery

-Increased critical damage

Completion bonus: Power +50

How to get it : The title is unlocked after maximizing the friendship with Dohalim.

WU XING COMMANDER (DLC)

-Enraged Luna Storm (Arte)

-Increased critical hits with Staff Extension

-Increased critical damage with Staff Extension

-Amplified attack with Staff Extension

-Increased duration of Staff Extension

Completion Bonus: Elemental Attack +50

How to get it : DLC

CONTEMPLATOR (DLC)

-Water Snake (Arte)

-JV refill at the beginning of the fight

-Increased bonus gauge gain after victory

-Increased gain of bonus gauge after victory

-JV refill at the beginning of the fight

Completion bonus : Elemental defense +50

How to get it : DLC

MAIN MODEL (DLC)

-Enchanted circle (Arte)

-Increased counterattack damage

-Increased critical strike rate on counterattack

-Increased counterattack critical strike rate

-Increased counterattack damage

Completion Bonus: Power +50

How to get it : DLC

The Artes

On this page of our complete Tales of Arise solution, you will find the list of all the Artes available for each character. In addition to the classic moves, you also have attacks called "Artes". These are the attacks that will allow you to make much more impressive and effective combos, cast spells, buffs, or heal yourself. If some Artes are learned naturally by advancing in the story or by leveling up, there are other ways to get new ones, such as by improving Arte mastery, or by buying them through your titles.

List of Artes d'Alphen

Arte	Arte Mastery	Element & direction	Burning edge
Devouring blade	Sword Strike	-	Infernal torrent
Demonic Fang	Sword Strike	-	Explosive circle
Sonic stabbing	Sword Strike	-	Tearing lightning
Lacerating wave	Sword Strike	Earth	Infernal torrent
Iron slicer	Sword Strike	-	Infernal torrent
Flight from the Wyvern	Sword Strike	- (Elevation)	Flight of the Phoenix
Destruction	Sword Strike	Earth	Tearing lightning

Lightning strike	Sword Strike	Light (Paralysis - Elevation)	Flight of the Phoenix
Rain of swords : alpha	Sword Strike	-	Tearing lightning
Wind cut	Sword Strike	Air (Elevation)	Burning Squall
Sovereign slash	Sword Strike	-	Burning wave
Double demonic fang	Sword Strike	-	Burning wave
Sonic stab 2	Sword Strike	-	Explosive circle
Eternal devastation	Sword Strike	Earth	Burning wave
Blades of nothingness	Sword Strike	-	Burning wave
Lightning Fang	Sword Strike	Light (Paralysis)	Explosive circle
Swarm of dragons	Sword Strike	-	Explosive circle
Howling Azure Storm (DLC)	Sword Strike	Water	Burning wave
Orochi's Frightful Fury (DLC)	Sword Strike	Air	Explosive circle
Plasma shock (CSD)	Sword Strike	Light (Paralysis - Elevation)	Burning Squall
Mirage	Air strike	- (Downhill)	Infernal torrent
Flight of the falcon	Air strike	- (Downhill)	Infernal torrent
Rondo luna	Air strike	-	Flight of the phoenix
Devastation	Air strike	-	Flight of the phoenix
Hurricane stab	Air strike	Air	Burning Squall
Stardust	Air strike	-	Flight of the phoenix
Lightning from nowhere	Air strike	Air	Burning Squall
Ascending light lance	Air strike	-	Flight of the phoenix
Devastation of the thunder	Air strike	Light (Paralysis)	Burning Squall
Infernal torrent	Flaming strike	Fire	Burning wave
Flight of the phoenix	Flaming strike	Fire	Burning wave
Explosive circle	Flaming strike	Fire	Burning wave
Tearing lightning	Flaming strike	Fire	Burning wave
Burning Squall	Flaming strike	Fire	Burning wave
Burning wave	Flaming strike	Fire	-
Scarlet explosion (Arte mystique)	Flaming strike	Fire	-
Incandescent pillar (Arte	Flaming strike	Fire	-

mystique)			

List of Artes de Shionne

In the Tales of series, in addition to the classic moves, you also have attacks called "Artes". These are the attacks that will allow you to make more impressive and efficient combos, to launch spells, buffs, or to heal yourself. If some Artes are learned naturally by advancing in the story or by leveling up, there are other ways to get new ones. Here is the list of Artes that Shionne can unlock.

Arte	Arte Mastery	Element & direction	Effect
First Aid	Arte astral	-	Lightly heals an ally's health
Circle of Care	Arte astral	-	Gradually restores the HP of allies in the circle's circumference
Revitalization	Arte astral	-	Restores the HP of all allies
Recovery	Arte astral	-	Heals the physical damage of an ally
Dissipation	Arte astral	-	Heals the physical alterations of all allies
Resurrection	Arte astral	-	Reanimate a knocked out ally
Large radius	Pustolet strike	-	-
Aquatic Gemini	Pustolet strike	Water	-
Lunar explosion	Pustolet strike	-	-
Lunar Corruption	Pustolet strike	-	-
Gravity field	Pustolet strike	Darkness (Curse)	-
Annihilation	Pustolet strike	Fire	-
Instant cyan (DLC)	Pustolet strike	Air	-
Ignis Celestra	Explosive strike	Fire	-
Ignis Diffus	Explosive strike	Fire	-
Tonitus Celestra	Explosive strike	Light (Paralysis)	-
Tonitus Pluvia	Explosive strike	Light (Paralysis)	-
Luke Celestra	Explosive strike	Light	-
Luke Divisio	Explosive strike	Light	-
Aranea Celestra	Explosive strike	Light (Paralysis)	-
Aranea Lubes	Explosive strike	Light (Paralysis)	-
Detonation	Frappe au pistolet	-	-
Toxicity	Frappe au pistolet	Darkness	-

		(Poison)	
Lance sweep	Frappe au pistolet	-	-
Scorched earth	Frappe au pistolet	Fire	-
Tres Ventos	Frappe au pistolet	Air	-
Aqueous impact	Frappe au pistolet	Water (Downhill)	-
Glacio Celestra	Explosive strike	Water (Gel)	-
Glacio Burst	Explosive strike	Water (Gel)	-
Volcanic strike	Arte astral	Fire	-
Flaming tornado	Arte astral	Fire	-
Explosion	Arte astral	Fire	-
Geyser	Arte astral	Water	-
Ice thrower	Arte astral	Water (Gel)	-
Ice Tornado (DLC)	Arte astral	Water (Gel)	-
Rayon (DLC)	Arte astral	Light	-
Devouring fire	Hitting with a gun	-	Arte mystique
Explosive charge	Hitting with a gun	-	Arte mystique

List of Artes de Rinwell

Arte	Arte Mastery	Element & direction	Effect
Concentration	Strike of light	-	Increases the power of an ally's strikes by 30%.
Acuity	Strike of light	-	Increases the elemental attack of an ally by 30%.
Rafale	Air Strike	Air	-
Photonic lightning	Strike of light	Light	-
Rising water	Water Strike	Water	-
Lightning orb	Strike of light	Light (Paralysis)	-
Thunderfield	Strike of light	Light (Paralysis)	-
Windy whirlwind	Air Strike	Air (Elevation)	-
Moisturizing orb	Air Strike	Water	-
Marteau céleste	Strike of light	Light (Paralysis)	-
Sharp Cyclone	Water Strike	Air	-
Flight of the	Water Strike	Air	-

swallow			
Electrical discharge	Strike of light	Light (Paralysis)	-
Ice Trap	Water Strike	Water (Gel)	-
Puddle	Water Strike	Water (Downhill)	-
Volcanic strike	Strike of light	Fire	-
Geyser	Water Strike	Water	-
Ice thrower	Water Strike	Water (Gel)	-
Rising tide	Water Strike	Water	-
Aerial stabbing	Air Strike	Air	-
Crossed blade	Air Strike	Air	-
Cyclone	Air Strike	Air	-
Thunder Blade	Strike of light	Light (Paralysis)	-
Sacred Spear	Strike of light	Light (Paralysis)	-
Divine sword	Strike of light	Light (Paralysis)	-
Maelstrom	Water Strike	Water	-
Shooting star	Strike of light	Light (Paralysis)	-
Storm of the Metrores	Strike of light	-	-
Burst of arrows (DLC)	Water Strike	Water	-
Croc de vent (DLC)	Air Strike	Air	-
Divine Ray (DLC)	Strike of light	Light (Paralysis)	-
Ecstatic divine roar	Strike of light	Light	Arte mystique
Aquarius Damnation	Water Strike	Water	Arte mystique

List of Artes de Dohalim

Arte	Arte Mastery	Element & direction	Effect
Care	Recovery	-	Restores an ally's HP
Healing	Recovery	-	Significantly restores an ally's health
Regeneration	Recovery	-	Gradually restores an ally's HP
Enchanted Circle	Recovery	Light	Quickly restores

(DLC)			the HP of allies in the circle's circumference
Dissipation	Recovery	-	Heals the physical alterations of all allies
Resurrection	Recovery	-	Reanimate a knocked out ally
Barrier	Recovery	-	Increases the defense and elemental defense of an ally by 30%.
Lion Heart	Recovery	-	Increases the JA recovery speed of an ally
Storm	Baton twirling	-	-
Catapult	Baton twirling	-	-
Lonely captivity	Baton twirling	Earth	-
Penumbra	Baton twirling	Earth (Elevation)	-
Elusive deity	Baton twirling	Darkness (Curse - Rise)	-
Seismic rupture	Baton twirling	Earth	-
Crescent lightning	Baton twirling	Air	-
Bloody flowers	Baton twirling	Darkness (Curse)	-
Raging Luna Storm (DLC)	Baton twirling	Air	-
Rotary hammer	Baton twirling	-	-
Tornado surge	Baton twirling	- (Downhill)	-
Sonic Lance	Baton twirling	-	-
Demon's spear	Baton twirling	Darkness (Curse)	-
Ascending wave	Baton twirling	Earth	-
Rage of the eagle	Baton twirling	- (Downhill)	-
Stalagmite	Demonic Strike	Earth	-
Gravisphere	Demonic Strike	Earth	-
Land Elk	Demonic Strike	Earth	-
Negative portal	Demonic Strike	Darkness (Curse)	-
Bloody howling	Demonic Strike	Darkness (Curse)	-
Execution	Demonic Strike	Darkness (Curse)	-
Water Snake (DLC)	Demonic Strike	Water	-

| Tectonic fission | Demonic Strike | - | Arte mystique |
| Temporal break | Demonic Strike | Darkness (Curse) | Arte mystique |

List of Artes de Law

Arte	Arte Mastery	Element & direction	Effect
Greenhouse Storm	Punching	-	-
Fangs	Punching	-	-
Dragon Throwing	Leg strike	- (Elevation)	-
Lightning tornado	Leg strike	Air	-
Techtonic punch	Punching	Earth	-
Low flame	Leg strike	Fire	-
Dance of the swallow	Leg strike	- (Elevation)	-
Lightning Mirage	Punching	-	-
Inspiration	Spirit	-	Restores some PV to Law
Steel	Spirit	-	Increases Law's attack and elemental attack by 30%.
Super swallow dance	Leg strike	-	-
Greenhouse Hurricane	Punching	- (Elevation)	-
Divine fang	Punching	-	-
Snake Fist (DLC)	Punching	Water (Elevation)	-
Dark Wind (DLC)	Leg strike	Air	-
Sparkling Wild Roar (DLC)	Punching	Light (Paralysis)	-
Eagle Loon	Leg strike	- (Downhill)	-
Sparkling Dragon	Leg strike	Air	-
Punch inferno	Punching	Fire	-
Bolero of fangs	Leg strike	-	-
Hegemonic blaze	Punching	Fire - (Descending)	-
Eagle Assault	Leg strike	- (Downhill)	-

Deadly chain of events	Leg strike	- (Downhill)	-
Dark claw of thunder	Leg strike	Light (Paralysis)	Arte mystique
Scarlet skies	Leg strike	Fire	Arte mystique

List of Artes de Kisara

Arte	Arte Mastery	Element & direction	Effect
Protective aura	Shield strike	Light	Heal an ally
Roar of the lion	Shield strike	-	Reinforced in case of custody
Burning Meteors	Powerful strike	-	-
Incendiary emission	Powerful strike	Earth	-
Tiger Blade	Shield strike	-	Reinforced in case of custody
Piercing roar	Shield strike	Light (Paralysis)	Reinforced in case of custody
Rolling Thunder	Shield strike	Earth	Reinforced in case of custody
Hurricane slice	Powerful strike	Air (Elevation)	-
Crescent moon	Shield strike	Earth	Reinforced in case of custody
Storm of wyvern	Shield strike	Air	Reinforced in case of custody
Crossfire	Powerful strike	Fire	-
Maximum explosion	Shield strike	Earth	Reinforced in case of custody
Slag attack	Shield strike	Earth	Reinforced in case of custody
Lunar Arc	Powerful strike	Earth	-
Ice bonfire	Shield strike	Water (Gel)	Reinforced in case of custody
Sadistic descent	Shield strike	- (Elevation)	-
Water snake groove (CSD)	Shield strike	Water	Reinforced in case of custody
Descending Storm (DLC)	Shield strike	Air	Reinforced in case of custody

			Reinforced in case of custody
Dazzling Spin (DLC)	Shield strike	Light	Reinforced in case of custody
Series of lightning bolts	Powerful strike	Air (Downhill)	-
Assault of the beast	Shield strike	-	-
Estocade of chaos	Powerful strike	-	-
Lance of light	Shield strike	-	-
Tearing storm	Shield strike	Air (Downhill)	-
Blizzard Flower	Shield strike	Water (Freezing - Descending	-
Fire demolisher	Shield strike	-	Arte mystique
Last hope	Shield strike	-	Arte mystique

K of the Killer's art is to to to improve his mastery of the Arte de la Ferreira... Improvements to the are made by and, the and time.

the list of trophies is available

Below is the list of 48 trophies (22 of which are hidden) for Tales of Arise, with our complete solution coming soon. The game is available on September 10 for PlayStation 5 and PlayStation 4 (34 bronze, 11 silver, 2 gold and 1 platinum).

BRONZE TROPHIES (34)

-Emissary of Liberation

Eliminate the lord Balseph. Raise your flag proudly. The battle has just begun.

-Conqueror of Darkness

Defeat Lord Ganabelt and restore hope to Cyslodia for the first time in centuries.

-Brothers in Arms

Recruit Lord Dohalim. With a friend like him, the Tournament of the Crown won't last long.

-Retired Avenger

Eliminate Lord Almeidrea. He's a boy who saved her from the revenge of one of her victims.

-Liberator of Dahna

Eliminate Lord Vholran. All Renian lords have been defeated, and Dahna is finally free.

-Invasion Stopped

Stop the lights emitted by the Anchor. Rena has already stolen too much from Dahna.

-Intertwined Hearts

Form a strong bond with Shionne, relive your first meal together and more if you like...

-An honest mage

Form a strong bond with Rinwell, and help her accept who she really is.

-Role model

Form a strong bond with Law, and give her a goal to strive for.

-A modest dream

Bond strongly with Kisara, and remind her to dream a little.

-Alcohol coma

Form a strong bond with Dohalim, and become the drinking buddy of an old lord.

Owls!

Find and report all the owls. Still, Hootle's place remains with Rinwell.

-Rebel Spark

Complete your first side quest. Even the smallest spark can turn into an inferno.

-Skilled Fisherman

Catch your first fish. It's not just a hobby, it's a means of survival.

-Instant Cooking

Cook your first dish. In these extreme conditions, the most important thing is to eat well.

-Armed to the teeth

Forge 100 types of weapons. This forging experience teaches you that every weapon has its purpose.

Jeweller

Craft 30 accessories. The eternal quest for the perfect balance between style and function.

-What a Name Says

Learn your first title skill (except DLC). Your name will become a source of power.

-100 Hit Combo

Inflict over 100 hits in one combo. Fight together and don't let your enemies fight back.

-Hit of the Century

Give it all you've got and inflict at least 10,000 points of damage in a single strike.

-Assiduous Counterattacker

Perform 100 counterattacks. Your enemies will be afraid to miss their attacks.

-Dilapidator

Spend 400000 Gald. In this team, items for sale don't stay that way for long.

-Almanac of Zeugles

Encounter 120 types of enemies (except DLC). Careful study will reveal their weaknesses.

-Eternal Fire

Eliminate Efrit Malum. Even a single spark can grow and consume the fiery colossus.

-Night Hatching

Eliminate Meneiys. If only you'd had time to admire the spectral flower a little more...

-Continental Earthquake

Eliminate the Giant Gnome. Its body was so gargantuan that even the ruins seemed tiny.

-Hurricane Blast

Eliminate Sylph Procella. The time you spent riding on his back will remain with you.

-Raging waves

Eliminate Ondine Luo. Even the most imposing opponent is no match for the power of the group.

-Big Game Hunter

Eliminate 20 giants. No adventurer can resist facing these beasts.

-Elite Frontline

Complete the ultimate training ground level. In this team, there's no need to train!

-Dilettante

Get your first artifact (except DLC). Its mesmerizing appearance never ceases to arouse curiosity.

-Novice Breeder

Collect your first crops on the ranch. Every life should be treated with love and respect.

-Owl Lover

Find and report 13 owls. We're starting to see glimpses of feathers in the lonely forest.

-Speech Mill

Watch 300 skits. Companions always find something to talk about.

-SILVER TROPHIES (11)

The Truth

Learn the truth about Dahna and Rena on Daeq Faezol. It's time to defeat the Great Spirit.

-Icebreaker

Form strong bonds with all your companions as a token of all the time spent together.

-Heroes of the People

Complete 70 side quests. No quest is too difficult for the team.

-Divine Fisherman

Catch all types of fish and show the Fishing Expert the fishing notes.

-Globetrotting Gourmet

Get 30 types of recipes (except DLC). The quest for gastronomy spans all of Dahna.

-Directory of Nicknames

Learn 400 title skills (except DLC). Fame comes with a myriad of nicknames.

-Apogee

Reach level 100, and the once outcast liberators of Dahna no longer fear anyone.

-Return to the Past

Complete "Memory Machine." Rivals from the past are no match for allies from the present.

-Curiosity Lover

Get 20 types of artifacts (excluding DLC). It's more than a collection, it's a calling.

-Veteran Breeder

Collect 50 crops on the ranch. The meat produced feeds the team and with it, their cause.

-Ornithologist

Find and report 32 owls. A chorus of hooting owls emerges from the forest.

GOLD TROPHIES (2)

-Born Liberator

Save the two planets from destruction. A bright future awaits the people of the new world.

-Survivor of the Otherworld

Complete the side quest "Visitors from Another World" and gather a certain duo.

PLATINUM TROPHY (1)

-Emergence

Proof of knowledge gained through many adventures and battles in both worlds.

Also read:

-Tales of Arise : An episode under the sign of renewal ?
-Tales of Arise : The game reveals details
-Tales of Arise : A last video tour before the release

END

Printed in Great Britain
by Amazon

67983124R00151